Lecture Notes in Computer Science 12451

More information about this subseries at http://www.springer.com/series/7409

In-Young Ko · Juan Manuel Murillo ·
Petri Vuorimaa (Eds.)

Current Trends in Web Engineering

ICWE 2020 International Workshops
KDWEB, Sem4Tra, and WoT4H
Helsinki, Finland, June 9–12, 2020
Revised Selected Papers

 Springer

Editors
In-Young Ko ⓘ
School of Computing
Korea Advanced Institute of Science
and Technology
Daejeon, Korea (Republic of)

Juan Manuel Murillo ⓘ
Escuela Politécnica
Universidad de Extremadura
Cáceres, Spain

Petri Vuorimaa
Department of Computer Science
Aalto University
Aalto, Finland

ISSN 0302-9743   ISSN 1611-3349   (electronic)
Lecture Notes in Computer Science
ISBN 978-3-030-65664-5   ISBN 978-3-030-65665-2   (eBook)
https://doi.org/10.1007/978-3-030-65665-2

LNCS Sublibrary: SL3 – Information Systems and Applications, incl. Internet/Web, and HCI

This Springer imprint is published by the registered company Springer Nature Switzerland AG
The registered company address is: Gewerbestrasse 11, 6330 Cham, Switzerland

Preface

The International Conference on Web Engineering (ICWE) aims to promote research and scientific exchange related to Web engineering, and to bring together researchers and practitioners from various disciplines in academia and industry in order to tackle emerging challenges in the engineering of Web applications and associated technologies, as well as to assess the impact of those technologies on society, media, and culture.

This volume collects the papers presented at the workshops co-located with the 20th International Conference on Web Engineering (ICWE 2020), virtually held during June 9–12, 2020, in Helsinki, Finland. In the tradition of previous ICWE conferences, the workshops complemented the main conference, and provided a forum for researchers and practitioners to discuss emerging topics, both within the ICWE community and at the crossroads with other communities. As a result, we accepted the following three workshops, whose papers included in this volume underwent a rigorous peer-review process. Due to the COVID-19 pandemic, all three workshops were held together virtually on June 9, 2020.

- First International Workshop on the Web of Things for Humans (WoT4H 2020)
- Second Semantics and the Web for Transport Workshop (Sem4Tra 2020)
- 6th International Workshop on Knowledge Discovery on the Web (KDWEB 2020)

The objective of the WoT4H workshop was to provide a forum for academics, industrial researchers, developers, and practitioners to discuss the challenges and advances in Internet of Things (IoT) and W3C Web of Things (WoT). The WoT4H 2020 (four papers) was specially focused on improving the interoperability and adaptation of smart devices to humans.

Sem4Tra 2020 (three papers) was an opportunity for disseminating and discussing use cases and studies showing the application of semantic and Web technologies in the transport domain. The workshop especially focused on providing a traveler with all the services needed for a door-to-door travel under a single payment whilst integrating disparate modes of mobility under one travel experience.

Finally, the main goal of KDWEB 2020 (one paper) was to provide a venue to researchers, scientists, students, and practitioners involved in the fields of Knowledge Discovery on Data Mining, Information Retrieval, and Semantic Web, for presenting and discussing novel and emerging ideas.

We would like to thank all the workshop organizers for their excellent work in identifying cutting-edge and cross-disciplinary topics in the rapidly moving field of Web engineering, and organizing inspiring workshops around them. A word of thanks also to the reviewers, for their meticulous work in selecting the best papers to be presented. Last, but not least, we would like to thank the authors who submitted their work to the workshops and all the participants who contributed to the success of these events.

June 2020

In-Young Ko
Juan Manuel Murillo
Petri Vuorimaa

Contents

6th International Workshop on Knowledge Discovery on the Web (KDWEB 2020)

First International Workshop
on the Web of Things for Humans
(WoT4H 2020)

First International Workshop on the Web of Things for Humans (WoT4H 2020)

Javier Berrocal[1] ⓘ, Martin Gaedke[2] ⓘ, Niko Mäkitalo[3] ⓘ,
and Mahda Noura[1] ⓘ

[1] University of Extremadura, Spain
mahda.noura@informatik.tu-chemnitz.de
[2] Chemnitz University of Technology, Germany
gaedke@informatik.tu-chemnitz.de
[3] University of Helsinki, Finland
niko.makitalo@helsinki.fi

Abstract. The IoT and WoT paradigms were conceived to make people's life easier by integrating different devices and adapting them to people's needs and preferences. The objective of the workshop WoT4H is to provide a forum for the discussion of challenges and advances in the integration and adaptation of smart devices to Humans.

Keywords: Web of Things · Internet of Things · Human in the loop

1 Introduction and Motivation

During the last few years the deployment of smart devices has been massive. This trend is expected to continue and even increase over the next few years. However, this deployment has also been fostered by specific companies creating closed environments. The Internet of Things (IoT) and W3C Web of Things (WoT) paradigms were conceived to make people's life easier by integrating different services and adapting them to people's needs and preferences. In these closed environments, this integration and adaptation becomes difficult or even impossible to achieve, greatly limiting the benefits of these paradigms.

This integration poses some questions that need further discussion by researchers: How can devices from different manufacturers be integrated? How can the data sensed/stored in different devices be integrated? How can that information be used to identify the users' preferences or activities? How could this information be used to adapt the smart devices' behavior?

WoT4H is a forum for academics, industrial researchers, developers, and practitioners to discuss the challenges and advances in IoT and WoT. The first edition of WoT4H was specially focused on improving the interoperability and adaptation of smart devices to Humans. Especially relevant for the workshop are the application of these paradigms and problems in real environments and situations, such as smart transportation, pollution, smart tourism, well-being, etc.

2 Presentations and Discussion

In the first edition of the workshop, four papers were selected for presentation. Two of them were selected as full papers and two as short papers.

The first paper, SOLID and PeaaS: Your Phone as a Store for Personal Data, written by Manuel Jesús-Azabal, Javier Berrocal, Sergio Laso, Juan Manuel Murillo, and José García-Alonso, presents the integration of the technology SOLID with the mobile computing model People as a Service in order to store user information in their mobile device and provide it to third parties.

The second paper, "Use of geolocation for the management of collective transport of people in stations and airports" (written by Antonio Sarasa Cabezuelo), proposes an Android mobile application that provides to both passengers and drivers the optimal route to a destination and makes it easier to hire that service.

The third paper, "Towards the Integration of Web of Things Applications based on Service Discovery," discusses a federated service discovery approach to support the management of WoT applications which ensures that the integration of the all the system's components can be addressed by following an SOA. The authors of this paper are Javier Criado, Juan Boubeta-Puig, Manel Mena, Juan Alberto Llopis, Guadalupe Ortiz, and Luis Iribarne.

Finally, the paper written by Daniel Flores-Martin, Javier Berrocal, Jose García-Alonso, and Juan Manuel Murillo (Extending W3C Thing Description to Provide Support for Interactions of Things in Real-Time) presents an extension of the W3C Thing Description to provide it with the ability to adapt the description and the interoperability of the devices to the situation at run-time. This allows devices to connect to each other being aware of the different situations they may be involved in to establish smarter and real-time communications.

The quality of the presented papers and their value is high, and the overall discussion provided by the authors within the workshop has shown the importance of the theme in the community of Web engineering.

3 Program Committee

Finally, we would like to thank all the members of the Program Committee for the work done and the high-quality reviews provided.

Juan Boubeta-Puig	University of Cádiz
Maria Ganzha	Warsaw University of Technology
Jose García-Alonso	University of Extremadura
Jaime Galán-Jiménez	University of Extremadura
Soumya Kanti Datta	EURECOM
Simon Mayer	University of St. Gallen and ETH Zurich

SOLID and PeaaS: Your Phone as a Store for Personal Data

Manuel Jesús-Azabal$^{(\boxtimes)}$, Javier Berrocal, Sergio Laso, Juan Manuel Murillo, and Jose Garcia-Alonso

QSEG, Universidad de Extremadura, Avda. Universidad S/N, 10003 Cáceres, Spain
{manuel,jberolm,slasom,juanmamu,jgaralo}@unex.es

Abstract. Advertising has become the most important source of income for a significant number of web-based companies. This income is usually dependent on the personal information that companies gather from their users which has led them to create very rich profiles of their users. However, these profiles do not follow any standard and are usually incomplete in the sense that users provide different subsets of information to each platform. Thus, the quality and quantity of the data varies between applications and tends to inconsistency. In this context, the SOLID initiative proposes an alternative to decentralize the user information giving them complete ownership of their information. In this demo, we propose a proof of concept in which SOLID is used to store the user information in their mobile device, following the People as a Service paradigm to provide this information as a service to third parties.

Keywords: SOLID · Mobile-centric architecture · Advertisement · Personal data · Smartphones

1 Introduction

Advertisement on the Internet is based on very specific targeting, so the right products are proposed to the appropriate public. Therefore, it is critical to identify user preferences and interests [1]. Moreover, corporations invest a lot of money in obtaining relevant data about their users. This background is used to better understand how to focus the marketing campaigns and advertisement of trademarks and products. Enterprises, like Facebook or Google, mainly base their business model on the management of this kind of information [2].

Companies using this business model are under the obligations imposed by the different personal data protection laws existing around the world. However, the potential of these companies to infer more complex information [3], which can be used for private ends or politics interests [4] is a current concern. Also, the lack of any storage standard implies that each enterprise maintains their own set of information, causing a big duplicity of resources. Additionally, data leaks suppose a potential threat for users who can find their data exposed. This problems were already brought to the public attention in cases like Cambridge

© Springer Nature Switzerland AG 2020
I.-Y. Ko et al. (Eds.): ICWE 2020 Workshops, LNCS 12451, pp. 5–10, 2020.
https://doi.org/10.1007/978-3-030-65665-2_1

Analytica [5]. An example of these problems can be music streaming platforms. A user that plays music 90% of the time in an application (e.g. Spotify) and 10% of the time in another (e.g. YouTube), would have accurate recommendations in the first one but poor in the second one. The user would also have two music listening profiles, each of them incomplete.

To address this, different projects are trying to establish an alternative model for personal data management. One of the most relevant works in this area is the SOLID initiative [6], a movement conceived by the World Wide Web ideator, Tim Berners-Lee. This project proposes the use of PODS (Personal Online Data Stores) to store personal information. Thus, external applications which require the information must be authorized by the PODS manager and they have to actively request the information.

In this demo, we present a prototype that integrates a SOLID PODS into a smartphone. This idea is based on the People as a Service (PeaaS) [7] paradigm. PeaaS propose to use smartphones as a virtual representation of their owners. Thus, the paper is organised as follows. First, Sect. 2 briefly describes some alternatives for massive data storage, explaining the relevance of SOLID and PeaaS. Second, Sect. 3 specifies the details about the presented demo and how the PODS is integrated to allow the smartphone to serve the user information as a service. Finally, Sect. 4 draws some conclusions about the paper.

2   Background and Related Work

The management and storage of personal information have elicited multiple works which try to bring transparency and control for the users. The SOLID initiative [6] is the most popular focused on personal information management, but it is not the only one which introduces an alternative models for data storage. There are also several works based on a distributed network where data storage is decentralized. Examples of these are [8–10] or [11].

The HAT project [8] (Hub of All Things) is similar to SOLID in the sense that it proposes a centralized entity to store the personal information. This centralized microserver provides the users' personal information. Thus, external applications consume the provided data without having to privately store it. It is a proposal which shares the purpose with SOLID, nevertheless, it is more centered on how to distribute the information with the external entities while HAT brings a model based on the combining, production and exchange of information.

Freenet [9] was originally born to fight censure and guarantee anonymous navigation. Thus, it distributes the information along with the network components, sharing bandwidth and storage space. Moreover, Freenet is based on the same principles as blockchain and support the delocalization of massive storage.

The Dat Foundation [10] promotes universal access and distribution of knowledge, avoiding data monopolies and private massive storage. The initiative has mainly boosted the Dat Protocol, which provides a peer-to-peer tool for dataset sharing. Furthermore, the system implements the tracking of data version [12], following the free software philosophy.

The Threefold Network [11] is an ecosystem for technology development which provides communication tools based on three main concepts: equality, freedom and sustainability. Thus, the project proposes a peer-to-peer model where data is only stored by the owner entity.

These three approaches bring alternative models for information storage and interactions between network elements. Nevertheless, the collaborative nature of the projects and the data scalability do not provide a concrete pattern to standardize personal information storage. SOLID is a proposal focused on changing the paradigm of data management and bringing real privacy to users. For that purpose, the users' personal information is kept in PODS, entities which work as a user profile and manage requests from external apps. The PODS is managed by the own user, who specifies the personal information and the applications which can access to this data. Thus, the user must approve external demands, becoming able to revoke the access anytime. As a result, personal information is separated from applications which must actively demand the data and remain authorized.

In this paper, we present a solution which integrates the SOLID philosophy into PeaaS [13], a paradigm that proposes the use of smartphones as a virtual representation of their owners. Due to the amount of sensors present in those devices and their pervasive presence in society they are the perfect tool to gather users information. Moreover, thanks to their computation capabilities, the user profiles gathered in smartphones can be used in a variety of ways.

Additionally, as detailed above, SOLID provides a solution to manage the user information in a single profile. This goal is perfectly aligned with the PeaaS paradigm, which needs a storage mechanism for the user virtual profile. Thus, this demo brings an integration between these two works, drawing on the possibilities of the smartphone. In the next section, we present an overview of the proposed solution and how external applications interact with the system.

3   Storing and Accessing SOLID Information in PeaaS

This paper proposes a proof of concept for personal data storage on smartphones using Solid under the PeaaS paradigm. The proposed solution deploys a PODS in a smartphone, serving as provider of the personal data to authorized applications which demand it. As a result, the personal information is stored in the user's device, managing external accesses and getting a full control of the data.

The proposed solution is based on two main elements: an smartphone, which serves the data and performs the storage process, authorization control and definition of the information; and an API gateway, an intermediate layer which is in charge of communicating the external requests with the user device.

The smartphone is in charge of executing a local SOLID PODS. This element is originally designed to be deployed in web servers. However, for this demo we have deployed it on an smartphone (technical details to replicate this demo can be found in[1]). Once this process is finished, the deployed application provides to

---

[1] https://bitbucket.org/spilab/solidsituational.context/src/master/.

the user all mechanisms to specify the personal information and manage external requests. To adapt the behaviour of the PODS to the PeaaS paradigm, it is necessary to install a PeeaS Application (also included in the above mentioned repository). This program will be in charge of executing a callback method in the smartphone when a call from the API Gateway is received. The API Gateway works as a common layer for all devices, providing the external request with the communication mechanism to reach the SOLID PODS. Figure 1 shows a step-by-step guide of the solution.

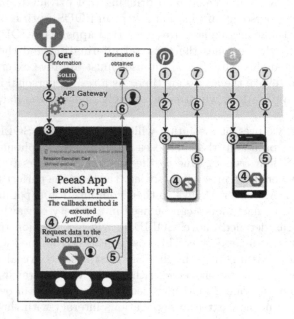

Fig. 1. Serving data from a smartphone based PODS.

The process begins when an external application requires information from the user. Since the data is stored in the local PODS, the API Gateway is in charge of communicating the request to the device. Thus, the process begins when the external application provides the individual SOLID domain of the data owner (1). Next, the API Gateway maps the SOLID domain with the corresponding device, notifying the request and waiting for the smartphone response (2). When the smartphone receives the notification (3), it executes a callback method in the PeeaS Application (4) which internally requests the personal data to the PODS deployed in the phone. When the personal profile information is obtained (5), the smartphone returns the data to the API Gateway (6), which responds to the external application (7). This way, the full communication process is completed. It is important to take into account the API Gateway is a common entity for all calls and interactions with the phones, becoming a relevant intermediate element.

Following this working scheme, an example case of use is explained in Fig. 2: Facebook wants to know the geolocalization position and interests of a concrete user to display custom advertisement. First, it is important that the user specifies Facebook as a friendly domain in the PODS, otherwise, the information request would not be allowed. This way, Facebook application knows the SOLID Domain of the user, value used to indicate the smartphone involved in the request. This variable is provided by the user when registration process is made. Thus, Facebook marks the GPS position and user interests set as desired information to the API Gateway, performing a GET petition and waiting for the response. Internally, the API Gateway maps the provided SOLID Domain and notifies the PeaaS application in the smartphone about the petition. Once the device is informed, authorization checks are made in the PODS. In the case the requester application is accepted, a callback method is executed and the SOLID PODS replies with the GPS position and interests set. As a result, the smartphone returns the data to the API Gateway, which provides Facebook with the demanded information. This working scheme is followed every time an external app requests a concrete data.

Fig. 2. Process to obtain GPS value and interests data from user PODS.

The proposed solution is based on the interoperation of multiple entities. As a result, the SOLID PODS works autonomously on the user smartphone, achieving a real separation between personal information and external applications. Thus, the governance of the data is entirely placed on the user. As a consequence, the personal information is managed by the user, becoming able to control the accesses from external parties.

4   Conclusions

Data governance has become an important issue, specially for online advertisement. Personal information has become an appreciated coin and enterprises invest important money amounts to obtain the users' personal information [1].

In this paper, a demo which joins the SOLID philosophy into the PeaaS paradigm has been provided. Therefore, smartphone devices become personal PODS for data storage. This way, the users keep the personal information on the phone and external applications must request it. Thanks to this, personal data is integrated into the individual device, allowing the user to keep a full control over the stored information and the access of external applications. Joining these two paradigms encourages a change of mind in privacy philosophy while providing a vanguard technological solution.

Acknowledgments. This work has been partially funded by the 4IE+ project (0499-4IE-PLUS-4-E) funded by the Interreg V-A España-Portugal (POCTEP) 2014–2020 program, by the Spanish Ministry of Science, Innovation and Universities (RTI2018-094591-B-I00), by the Department of Economy and Infrastructure of the Government of Extremadura (GR18112, IB18030), and by the European Regional Development Fund.

References

1. Ruckenstein, M., Granroth, J.: Algorithms, advertising and the intimacy of surveillance. J. Cult. Econ. **13**(1), 12–24 (2020)
2. Fuchs, C.: The political economy of privacy on facebook. Telev. New Media **13**(2), 139–159 (2012)
3. Matz, S.C., Menges, J.I., Stillwell, D.J.: Andrew Schwartz, H: Predicting individual-level income from facebook profiles. PLoS ONE **14**(3), e0214369 (2019)
4. Benson, V., Buchanan, T.: Social big data and its integrity: the effect of trust and personality traits on organic reach of facebook content. In: Cyber Influence and Cognitive Threats, pp. 145–158. Elsevier (2020)
5. ur Rehman, I.: Facebook-Cambridge analytica data harvesting: what you need to know. Libr. Philos. Pract., 1–11 (2019)
6. The SOLID Foundation. The solid project. https://solid.mit.edu. Accessed 27 Feb 2020
7. Guillen, J., et al.: People as a service: a mobile-centric model for providing collective sociological profiles. IEEE Softw. **31**(2), 48–53 (2013)
8. Ng, I.C.L.: Can you own your personal data? The hat (hub-of-all-things) data ownership model (2018)
9. Clarke, I., Sandberg, O., Wiley, B., Hong, T.W.: Freenet: a distributed anonymous information storage and retrieval system. In: Federrath, H. (ed.) Designing Privacy Enhancing Technologies. LNCS, vol. 2009, pp. 46–66. Springer, Heidelberg (2001). https://doi.org/10.1007/3-540-44702-4_4
10. The DAT Foundation. The dat foundation. https://dat.foundation. Accessed 15 Apr 2020
11. The Threefold Network. The threefold network. https://threefold.io. Accessed 15 Apr 2020
12. Ogden, M., McKelvey, K., Madsen, M.B., et al.: Dat-distributed dataset synchronization and versioning. Open Sci. Fram. **10** (2017)
13. Berrocal, J., Garcia-Alonso, J., Canal, C., Murillo, J.M.: Situational-context: a unified view of everything involved at a particular situation. In: Bozzon, A., Cudre-Maroux, P., Pautasso, C. (eds.) ICWE 2016. LNCS, vol. 9671, pp. 476–483. Springer, Cham (2016). https://doi.org/10.1007/978-3-319-38791-8_34

Use of Geolocation for the Management of Collective Transport of People in Stations and Airports

Antonio Sarasa Cabezuelo(✉) iD

Universidad Complutense de Madrid Spain, Calle Profesor José García Santesmases, 9,
28040 Madrid, Spain
asarasa@ucm.es

Abstract. Airports have become a widely used form of transportation, and communication from the airport to cities is key. In this sense, a common problem that
passengers encounter when they arrive at the airport is finding a way to get to
the city. There are several alternatives such as metro, taxi, bus or train. However,
in recent years shuttle buses have emerged. It is a private bus that transports a
small number of people so that the cost of the trip is shared by all passengers.
The main problem with this transport is calculating the most optimal route for
passenger stops so that they reach their destinations as soon as possible. This
problem is exacerbated when the city is large. Generally the driver calculates the
route based on his experience or aided by a geographic route application. However in these cases, it must calculate the routes one by one. This work presents an
Android mobile application that implements a service aimed at managing this type
of transport, in a way that makes it easier for the passenger to contract a service
online. On the other hand, it makes it easier for the driver to find the optimal route
of stops using the information of the destinations registered by the passengers and
the geolocation information of the driver's mobile.

Keywords: Geolocation · Optimization · App Android

1 Introduction

Airports have become strategic centers of economic activity and it is essential for cus-
tomers to have an efficient mobility network. In this sense, a daily problem for people
traveling is finding a means of transportation that will take them from the airport to their
destination in the city. For this, it has several alternatives such as buses, metro, taxi or
train. However, in recent years, one of the most used services is the shuttle. A shuttle [3]
is a small private bus whose objective is to transport a set of users from the airports to
different destinations that users have previously chosen to end the journey at the point
of origin. The advantage of this transport is that it is generally cheaper than using an
individual taxi because the cost is shared among all users. Most companies in charge of
managing this type of services have branches in the airports themselves to contract these

© Springer Nature Switzerland AG 2020
I.-Y. Ko et al. (Eds.): ICWE 2020 Workshops, LNCS 12451, pp. 11–23, 2020.
https://doi.org/10.1007/978-3-030-65665-2_2

services. In this sense, the user normally contracts the Shuttle service at the airport upon arrival.

However, this transport presents a problem that is finding the optimal route so that users can reach destinations as soon as possible [6]. In many cases, the route is based on the experience of the driver who dynamically decides the order of stops to follow [1]. Although the driver could also use a geographical application to search the routes one by one according to the order of stops that the driver has decided to do. In order to solve this problem, there are a large number of applications that allow calculating the optimal route from a place to a destination, such as Google maps and similar applications. However, these applications do not take into account the particularity of having to do several stops and therefore the need of set an order of how to carry out these stops [4]. Formally it corresponds to the traveling salesman problem, which raises the problem about how to travel to a set of cities and visit them only once if it is known the distances between them. However, in the problem presented, in addition to the distances between the destinations, other aspects to optimize the route must also be considered [5], such as the events that may arise dynamically on the journey [2]. Another aspect that must be taken into account is the fact that if a city has large dimensions, and the Shuttle service covers the entire city, then the destinations of the travelers may be very far from each other, so the route will be long [7].

The use of sensors in the daily life of citizens is expanding more and more, so that the advantages of the Internet of Things become more evident. For example, it is common to use smart watches that are capable of measuring the main physical constants in athletes, the use of sensors at home to control the temperature of the house or light levels … In this article, it is described an Android mobile application that has been developed to solve the problem presented using geolocation and the establishment of restricted geographical areas to perform the service.

First, the app organizes the service by establishing geographical limits where shuttles can do stops. These limits are defined using the postal code configured by the driver of the shuttle. In this way, the driver publishes the geographical area in which is offered the service limiting the possible routes. The objective of this limitation is to ensure that the destinations where the shuttle will have to stop are not too far from each other. On the other hand, the app manages directly the hiring of the shuttle service. In this sense, the traveler must request the service from the app. In the contracting process, the traveler must provide the exact destination. In this way, the app will dispose all the destinations before the trip. Using this data and the location of the airport, the app calculates the optimal route of stops to be carried out so that users arrive at their destinations as soon as possible. Furthermore, this route is recalculated to take into account possible dynamically occurring events such as accidents, traffic or any other circumstance. There are applications similar to the one presented in this article such as Uber, Cabify, or MyTaxi. They have in common that it allows to contract a shared or non-passenger transport service using a mobile application. In addition, in all cases there is a version of the application for passengers and another for drivers, where it is possible to configure aspects such as the type of car, the type of music to listen to on the journey…

The article is structured in the following way. Section 2 shows the architecture and data model used. Section 3 presents the functionality developed. Next, Sect. 4 describes the results obtained from a usability evaluation carried out with real users. Finally, Sect. 5 presents a set of conclusions and lines of future work.

2 Architecture and Data Model

2.1 Technology and Arquitecture

In order to implement this application, the following technology has been used to implement this architecture:

1. Android for the development of the mobile application.
2. Firebase to implement the database. It offers services that facilitate the implementation of web and mobile applications. Among other services:

   - Realtime database/Cloud firestore: stores and synchronizes the data in one of these two databases in the JSON format. In addition, it is possible to add triggers for different types of requests.
   - Authentication: service that facilitates the login and its management.
   - Cloud Storage: it allows the storage and download of files from an application.
   - Cloud functions: it is in charge of managing the server code executed when an https request is received.

3. Mapbox is an online map provider that allows to render and manage maps. Its main features: it allows to customize the rendering of the maps and all their components, obtain coordinates from an address, geolocate the mobile phone or calculate an optimal route that passes through various points. It offers an API to access its services.

The application architecture follows a client-server model. The role of the client is played by an Android application from which it interacts with the server through https requests. The server offers a set of services implemented using node.js. Also through the server information is retrieved from the database. Figure 1 shows the architecture schematic.

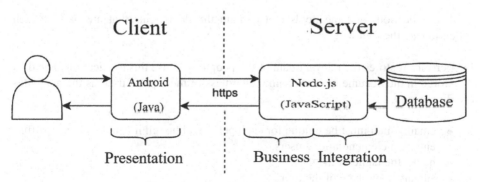

Fig. 1. Architecture of the application.

A critical element in the operation of the application is how to calculate the optimal route. For this the application takes two sources of information. On the one hand, it takes the geolocation of the driver and the coordinates where the destinations of the passengers are located. From this data, it makes a request to the API of the Mapbox site, which calculates in real time which is the best route to make stops at the passengers' destinations. Once the journey begins, the system recalculates the route for any event that could affect the journey.

2.2 Datamodel

The data model has been implemented using a NoSQL Firebase database. In this sense, the following organization has been defined (see Fig. 2):

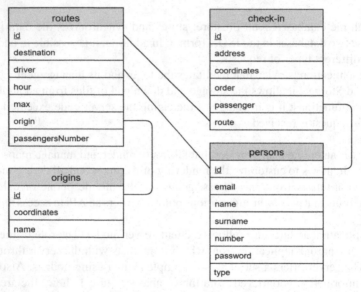

Fig. 2. Structure of database

The collections and the fields that contain the documents that are part of each collection are the following:

1) persons: it stores the relevant data of the people who use this application. The data stored in the documents is the same regardless of the type of user, as the attributes do not vary.

  - email: email must be unique for each person, although it is not used as a differentiating element among users.
  - name: the name of the user.
  - surname: surname of the user.
  - number: telephone number.

- password: password required to enter the application.
- type: user type of the application: "passenger", "driver" and "admin". This attribute is used to know if a certain user has permission to do a certain request or to access a specific view.

2) origins: it stores the origins entered by the administrator.

- coordinates: the coordinates of the origin.
- name: the name of the street, square, terminal… from where the bus will depart.

3) routes: Contains information on current routes.

- destination: It is specified with the postal code. The driver chooses the postal code of the area where it will do the stops. In this way, passengers whose destination is within that code may be included in the trip.
- driver: id of the driver who will make the journey.
- hour: it is the departure time. This attribute is used so that, once the passenger has selected an origin and a destination, a list with all the journeys with the departure times is displayed and the passenger can choose the most convenient one.
- max: maximum number of passengers that the shuttle bus can take. When the current number of passengers equals this number, no further reservations are allowed.
- origin: id of the origin of the route.
- passengersNumbers: number of passengers who have registered for the trip.

4) check-in: It saves the inscriptions that passengers do when adding themselves to a journey. Using this table, it is possible to recover the trips to which a passenger is registered.

- address: full address where the passenger wants to get off.
- coordinates: coordinates of the place where the passenger wants to get off.
- order: position on the bus list.
- passenger: passenger's id.
- route: id of the route to which the passenger has registered.

Note that to organize the data and avoid inconsistencies, the ids automatically generated by Firestore are used as identifiers. In most cases it is used to reference data between different collections. However, in the case of collection of "Check-in" it could be dispensed with and in the collection of persons the email could have been used, but the id was used as a reference to facilitate the modification of the email and avoid a conflict in the relationships between the data.

3 Functionality

The application supports several roles, so the functionalities of each role will be explained in the following sections.

3.1 Administrator

The administrator is responsible for establishing the points of origin from which drivers and passengers will choose to start their route. The main administrator interface consists of two parts (see Fig. 3a and b): the first contains a map and a search bar from which an origin point is entered. The second part of the interface is a text editor in which the name of the new origin is entered.

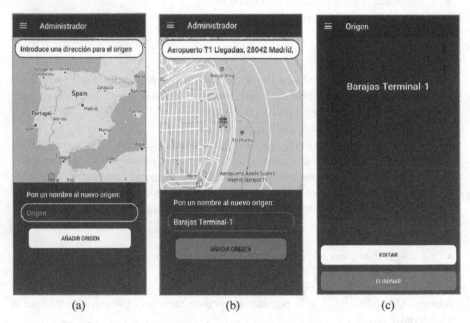

(a)   (b)   (c)

Fig. 3. a. Administrator interface, b. Selection origin, c. Origin interface.

Once the previous steps have been completed, the process is finished by clicking on the add button ("AÑADIR ORIGEN"). If the origin has been added correctly, it is redirected to an interface where two actions can be performed (see Fig. 3c): click on the delete button ("ELIMINA") to delete the created origin, or click on the edit button ("EDITAR") that allows modifying the origin name.

At the top left of the main administrator interface is a menu with various functions (see Fig. 4a): the start button ("Inicio") that redirects to the main interface, the origins button ("Origenes") that allows access to a list (see Fig. 4b) of all available origins (if it is clicked on any from them, it is accessed the origin functions described above), the user account settings button ("Ajustes") and the logout button ("Cerrar Sesión").

3.2 Driver

The driver is responsible for creating new routes so that passengers can hire them. The main driver interface (see Fig. 5a) consists of a form in which the data corresponding to

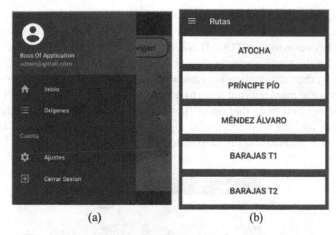

(a)   (b)

Fig. 4. a. Administrator's menu, b. List of origins registered.

the route to be taken must be entered: the point of origin pre-established by the administrator, the postal code where the service will be offered to passengers, the maximum capacity of people that can be carried in the vehicle and the departure time from the starting point. Once all the data has been entered, the process ends by clicking on the create route button ("CREAR TRAYECTO"). If the data is incorrect, a warning message is displayed and if the data is correct, the new path is created and redirected to the main interface.

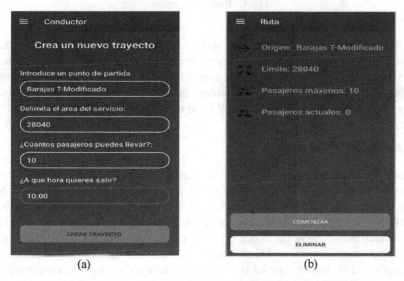

(a)   (b)

Fig. 5. a. Main driver interface, b. Interface of route created.

This interface (see Fig. 5b) shows the route information and several options: a button to delete ("ELIMINAR") the route (as long as the route does not contain customer requests) and the option to start ("COMENZAR") the route (only accessible if the number of passengers for the route is greater than or equal to 1). If it is clicked on the option to start the journey, then the application retrieves the destinations to be performed by the driver, calculates the most optimal route to reach them using the Mapbox API and shows on the map the optimal route that passes through all stops. Next, it offers the option to start the journey and the map zoom (see Fig. 6) will point to the position on the map where the driver is located and begin to follow the movements.

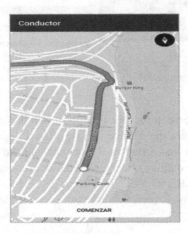

Fig. 6. Route of journey.

At the top left there is a menu with several options (see Fig. 7a): the start button ("Inicio") from which it is possible to access the main driver interface, the routes button ("Rutas") that allows to access a list of the available routes (see Fig. 7b) that the driver has at that time (if it is clicked on any of the routes you access the options mentioned above), the user account settings button ("Ajustes") and the logout button ("Cerrar Sesión").

3.3 Client

The passenger is the user who contracts the journey published by the driver. The main passenger interface (see Fig. 8a) consists of a map that shows the user's geolocation and through which it is possible to navigate. At the top of this map, there are two search bars in which the passenger must enter a point of origin (already preset) and the destination point to which they want to go. When it is entered the origin, a bus icon is added to the map in the coordinates of the indicated address, and when the destination is entered a finish flag is added. In both cases it is zoomed so that the passenger can make sure that the address is correct.

When the user types, suggestions for auto-completion appear. To do this, for each complete word entered by the user, a request is launched through the Mapbox API that returns a list with the addresses that match the word inserted by keyboard. This list is the

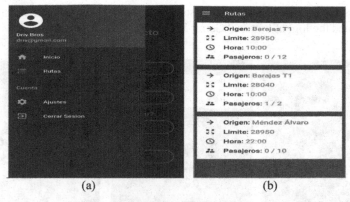

Fig. 7. a. Menu, b. List of the available routes

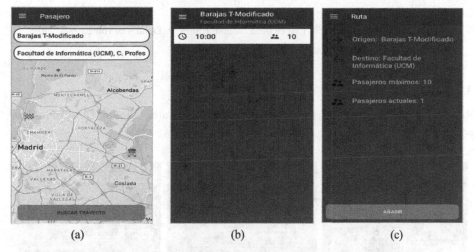

Fig. 8. a. Main passenger interface, b. List of bus routes, c. Details of route.

one used in autocompleting. Likewise, in the same request, the coordinates that will be used to mark the map and calculate the route and the postal code with which the routes will be searched are obtained.

Once both steps have been completed, click on the search route button ("BUSCAR TRAYECTO") that shows a list with the different bus routes at different times (see Fig. 8b) that are available according to the data entered. Once a route has been chosen from the list, its details are shown (see Fig. 8c) and the option to contract the trip is found by clicking on the add button ("AÑADIR").

At the top left there is a menu with several options (see Fig. 9a): the start button ("Inicio") from which it is possible to access the main driver interface, the routes button ("Rutas") that allows to access a list of the routes (see Fig. 9b) contracted by the passenger (if it is clicked on a route from the list, the information of that route is displayed together with the possibility of canceling a route (see Fig. 9c)), the user account settings button ("Ajustes") and the logout button ("Cerrar Sesión").

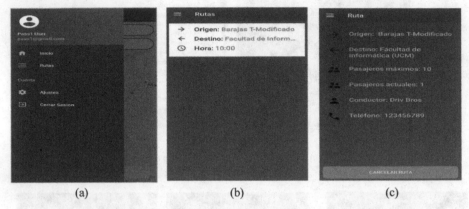

(a)   (b)   (c)

Fig. 9. a. Menu, b. List of the available routes, c. Details of route.

3.4 Other Interfaces

Regardless of the type of user, there are a set of screens that are common. These interfaces are (see Fig. 10):

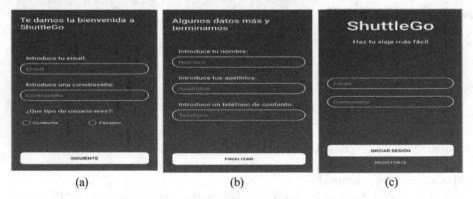

(a)   (b)   (c)

Fig. 10. a. Register, b. Register, c. Login

- Main screen. In it the user must authenticate himself by entering the username and password.
- Registration screen. In it the user must enter the email, the contact telephone number, the name and surname, the user and password to authenticate themselves in the application and the type of user. It is only possible to register with a type of conduit or passenger user. The administrator user type has its own username and password.

4 Evaluation

The usability of the application has been evaluated among a group of 20 people where 70% were between 19 and 35 years of age, and the remaining 30% were over 36 years of age. The evaluation consisted of carrying out a set of tasks on the application: log in as a driver, register a new route, cancel the previously created trip, start a journey with passengers, register as a new passenger, search for a trip as a passenger and book, and cancel the reservation previously made. After taking the tests, the respondents had to answer a set of questions regarding the usability of the application. The evaluation process was carried out using Google Forms. In all cases, the scores are on a scale of 0 to 5, with 5 being the highest satisfaction and 0 being the worst grade. The main questions asked were about:

- Utility of the application. 13 have responded that their satisfaction level is 4, on the other hand, 2 people have given a score of 3 and the remaining 5 have assessed with the highest score.
- Ease of use of the application. The maximum score has been voted by 7 of the total, while 5 people have scored 5. The remaining 8 answers have given a rating of 4 points.
- Application design. 55% of respondents find it an aspect that is "very good". 25% have responded that the design is "good", while the remaining 20% have rated with the highest score.
- Global assessment. 55% of respondents responded "very well". The percentage of score "excellent" has increased to 30% and the remaining percentage has rated the application with "good".

Figure 11 shows the result of the evaluation.

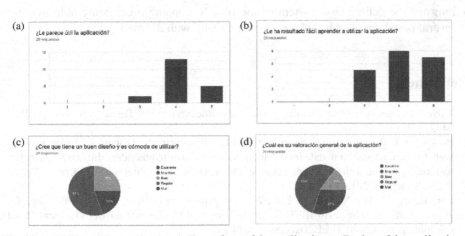

Fig. 11. a. Utility of the application, b. Ease of use of the application, c. Design of the application, d. Global assessment.

5   Conclusions and Future Work

An Android application for the management of shuttle bus services has been created. Among the advantages it offers from the passenger's point of view is that it has the possibility of contracting the service online from a mobile application. In this sense, the passenger only needs to enter an origin and a destination, and the shuttles that will make that route will be shown, along with their departure time. From the driver's point of view, an application is available to help you organize the journey that you should take in an optimal way according to the destinations that passengers have registered. In this sense, the driver will automatically be shown the route to follow as soon as the number of passengers has been completed. Likewise, the application helps the driver to organize his service by being able to configure the area for carrying out stops and the schedule for carrying out the service.

The main lines of future work are:

- Implement an encryption system for users' personal information.
- Establish a price system for each journey and an online payment method.
- Add more functionality to facilitate the estimated time of a journey or to find out which journeys are at a certain time.
- Establish a notification system that keeps users informed of events related to their journeys.
- Improve the delimitation system of the route's stopping area, being able to enter several postal codes or be able to interact directly with the map.
- Implement an encryption system for users' personal information
- Establish a price system for each journey and an online payment method.
- Establish a notification system that keeps users informed of events related to their journeys.
- Improve the delimitation system of the route's stopping area, being able to enter several postal codes or be able to interact directly with the map.

References

1. Jerby, S., Ceder, A.: Optimal routing design for shuttle bus service. Transp. Res. Rec. **1971**(1), 14–22 (2006)
2. Pholprasit, T., Pongnumkul, S., Saiprasert, C., Mangkorn-ngam, S., Jaritsup, L.: LiveBusTrack: high-frequency location update information system for shuttle/bus riders. In: 2013 13th International Symposium on Communications and Information Technologies (ISCIT), pp. 565–569. IEEE, September 2013
3. Liu, Y., Jia, G., Tao, X., Xu, X., Dou, W.: A stop planning method over big traffic data for airport shuttle bus. In: 2014 IEEE Fourth International Conference on Big Data and Cloud Computing, pp. 63–70. IEEE, December 2014
4. Lu, J., Yang, Z., Timmermans, H., Wang, W.: Optimization of airport bus timetable in cultivation period considering passenger dynamic airport choice under conditions of uncertainty. Transp. Res. Part C Emerg. Technol. **67**, 15–30 (2016)
5. Yim, Y.B., Ceder, A.: Smart feeder/shuttle bus service: consumer research and design. J. Public Transp. **9**(1), 5 (2006)

6. Yue, W.S., Chye, K.K., Hoy, C.W.: Towards smart mobility in urban spaces: bus tracking and information application. In: AIP Conference Proceedings, vol. 1891, no. 1, p. 020145. AIP Publishing LLC, October 2017
7. Zhou, P., Zheng, Y., Li, M.: How long to wait? Predicting bus arrival time with mobile phone based participatory sensing. In: Proceedings of the 10th International Conference on Mobile Systems, Applications, and Services, pp. 379–392, June 2012

Towards the Integration of Web of Things Applications Based on Service Discovery

Javier Criado[1](✉) [ID], Juan Boubeta-Puig[2] [ID], Manel Mena[1] [ID],
Juan Alberto Llopis[1] [ID], Guadalupe Ortiz[2] [ID], and Luis Iribarne[1] [ID]

[1] Applied Computing Group, University of Almeria, Almería, Spain
{javi.criado,manel.mena,jallopis,luis.iribarne}@ual.es
[2] Department of Computer Science and Engineering, University of Cadiz,
Cádiz, Spain
{juan.boubeta,guadalupe.ortiz}@uca.es

Abstract. The current state of the technologies related to the Web of Things (WoT) and the Internet of Things (IoT) fosters the creation of service directories gathering resource descriptions. These directories are aimed at enabling the service discovery and supporting providers and consumers with a shared element for their communication and interoperability between the involved agents. This interoperability can be ensured by using the abstract layer of the W3C WoT recommendations. However, many of the existing approaches do not include a service discovery mechanism and those that include a WoT directory lack certain functionalities required by distributed systems specific to the WoT such as a Service-Oriented Architecture (SOA). This paper proposes a federated service discovery approach to support the management of WoT applications which ensures that the integration of the whole system components can be addressed by following a SOA. It is aimed at providing query and storage functionality for WoT resources, but also is intended to be connected to other WoT directories by applying a customizable approach based on recommender systems. Thus, we guarantee a flexible mechanism to obtain sets of ranked WoT resources to be utilized in different kinds of applications and domains.

Keywords: Web of Things · Service discovery · Interoperability · Federation · Integration · Service-Oriented Architecture

1 Introduction

The increasing number of Internet of Things (IoT) devices encourages the development of solutions focused on solving the interoperability and integration of such systems [1]. In this sense, communication mechanisms should be provided to enable the connection between devices by obtaining the required responses from the different service requests. It is key that this communication must deal with the heterogeneity of the protocols and technologies used in the IoT domain. With this aim, W3C Recommendations of the Web of Things (WoT) provide an

I.-Y. Ko et al. (Eds.): ICWE 2020 Workshops, LNCS 12451, pp. 24–29, 2020.
https://doi.org/10.1007/978-3-030-65665-2_3

abstract layer to make the communications and descriptions uniform under web standards and technologies [2,3].

The discovery of services related to IoT devices can be used to facilitate the execution of communication tasks, thus enabling the interoperability [4]. In this sense, middlewares, registries and service directories have proven useful for service discovery in Service-Oriented Architectures (SOA) [5]. Moreover, current cloud and multi-cloud approaches utilize modern service directories to connect their resources [6].

This way, dynamic changes in the availability of services and resources can be managed by a common element that centralizes the publishing and discovering features. Therefore, all kinds of consumer agents (developers, managers, applications, etc.) are able to obtain the information that describes the resources provided by the system, and to execute any available service.

Nevertheless, the existence of a sole element for publishing, consuming and managing the discovery of WoT resources may cause some additional problems, such us reducing the performance due to bottlenecks, increasing the complexity on management tasks because of the directory size, or avoiding dynamic addition of a complete set of services from a new source. Furthermore, development teams may require a proper (internal or external) service directory that facilitates the management, for instance, by providing its own processes for describing and registering new resources. Due to these reasons, federated approaches of directories are a suitable solution for enabling the service discovery [7].

This paper presents an approach based on a federated discovery service mechanism to support the management of WoT resources and facilitate the integration of WoT applications. This mechanism is intended to provide the following functionalities: (a) storing the WoT descriptions in a standardized format conforming the W3C recommendations, (b) providing register and query operations to allow the execution of publishing and consuming actions on the directory, (c) managing the different sources of the directory by linking different discovery services, and (d) using recommender objects [8] to both enable the configuration of the query policies and filter the results by adapting the responses depending on the request context.

The rest of the paper is organized as follows. Section 2 describes the approach for integrating WoT applications by using a federated discovery service. Section 3 pointed out some open challenges that are identified during the development of the approach. Section 4 reviews the related work and, finally, Sect. 5 outlines the conclusions and proposes the future work.

2   Approach

The main goal of our approach is focused on the definition of a service discovery mechanism to be applied in the WoT domain for the integration of applications. It must ensure the finding of WoT resources and should have into account the interoperability, flexibility and other quality factors of services. For these reasons, our discovery service is intended to include the following features.

In the first place, the service discovery mechanism should be federated by linking different discovery services (see Fig. 1). This way, if a client agent looks up information by inquiring a discovery service that is not able to solve the request, the query can be delegated and spread to other discovery services in order to arrange a greater space for the identification and classification of WoT resources (*things*). Thus, the proposed discovery mechanism would allow us to identify, classify and connect the available entities and, furthermore, it will enable the discovery through a network of federated services.

The approach will include different strategies of querying the federated discovery services. A possible alternative is to combine breadth and depth searching techniques for increasing the query levels on the one hand (by taking into account the linked discovery services), and examining the own data structure for each discovery service on the other hand.

In the second place, our approach must deal with the correct construction of the queries. A service request could obtain an empty result because of different causes, for example, an incomplete statement or a wrong condition. For this reason, we will apply query mutation techniques for modifying this kind of requests, thus obtaining variations that do allow to discover some WoT entities or resources. We will also analyze the potential utilization of query schemes aimed at specifying what types of data are expected to be obtained as a result, for example, applying a GraphQL-based approach.

The third feature that our approach includes is the consideration of semantic information as part of the service discovery process. In this sense, WoT recommendations include semantic information for the definition of *things* through the use of ontologies or taxonomies. Therefore, a discovery service can take this information into account to calculate metrics and matching values between an input specification and the possible output specifications that fully or partially comply with the requirements.

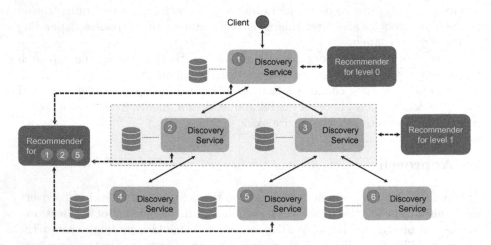

Fig. 1. Federated discovery services and recommender systems for WoT resources

Depending on the established matching conditions, a discovery service may consider a particular service to be a candidate satisfying the search criteria in part or in whole of the specification. The criteria established to consider a match as sufficient is related to the information quality managed by the discovery service and associated with WoT resources' specifications. As a consequence, our approach includes the use of quality models and standards (*e.g.*, ISO/IEC 25012) to establish the quality requirements, describe the metrics to be applied and evaluate the quality of the data managed by the discovery services.

Based on a client request and taking the aforementioned matching conditions into account, a discovery service offers in response a list of WoT resources that meet the established specifications. This list can be sorted or filtered to enable the selection of the best alternative, and this selection can be based on the client preferences, the logged usage or the configuration of the application domain, among other possible examples. With this aim, our approach incorporates the use of recommenders to calculate the best alternatives during the service discovery. Recommeder subsystems can be deployed as a part of the discovery service or as a separated service, and can be in charge of (*i*) a specific discovery service, (*ii*) the services of a level, or (*iii*) a custom set of discovery services (Fig. 1).

3   Challenges

A set of challenges that must be addressed during the development of the proposed service discovery mechanism have been identified. The main goal of this service discovery is to find the most appropriate WoT resources maximizing the search space and the performance, but this kind of federated discovery processes could have some limitations. For example, the greater the search depth, the greater the latency time in the search for services, or the network overload.

One possible solution to the performance problem is to form a peer-to-peer network of discovery services to decrease the latency rate and be able to respond more quickly to the requests [9]. Regarding the network overload, we are evaluating some cache-based and offline approaches for reducing the remote communications. Another solution could be based on heuristics to optimize the query process into the search spaces [10]. Therefore, a trade-off mechanism should be in charge of balancing the query conditions depending on the context situations.

The configuration of this mechanism should be based on policies and rules being expressive enough, but allowing a simple and dynamic management. Furthermore, the access to the discovery services must avoid the creation of a bottleneck due to a great number of concurrent requests directed to a common shared point for discovering the available WoT resources.

Another shortcoming could be finding real WoT entities accessible to the public domain. Our approach's utility depends on the existence of multiple discovery services with a large number of real components offering similar operations.

Finally, the evaluation of the obtained results with regard to other existing approaches could involve systems with different models for the description of things, different query formats, or not comparable structures of returned types.

4 Related Work

Search and discovery techniques are used as a bridge between users and cyber-physical systems, but also as a middleware for the interconnection of any agent related to the WoT domain [11]. This kind of mechanisms are aimed at enabling the search for entities and their resources, i.e., services and data [12].

In the WoT Store solution [13], the authors propose a system for the distribution, discovery and installation of WoT applications. It includes a semantic search engine capable of discovering things (and applications compatible with them) through the use of a web portal capable of handling SPARQL queries. The approach of WoT Store has some parallelism with mobile application markets, like searching over a software catalog, or downloading and installing code directly from the store. Our approach introduces the federation of different stores (directories) and the capability to decide what resource is more appropriate.

In [14], the authors present Dyser, a real-time search engine for WoT entities that supports the search for changes of the information generated by sensors. WoTSF [15] establishes an approach based on two different levels. The first level is a global search engine that divides the queries in different subqueries. These subqueries are processed in the second level formed by one or more individual local search engines (WoTSEs), thus providing fast queries to look up a specific type of resource in a local directory. The global search engine only aggregates the information stored at the master index, and it builds the appropriate requests to the APIs in parallel to retrieve accurate results. This step could increase the search time and our approach tries to solve this problem by implementing a federated search mechanism based on recommenders that limits the propagation of the query process depending on the requirements and the context information.

Other existing approaches use simpler mechanisms based on DNS or bluetooth technologies for broadcasting the addresses of the resources, as in the case of the Mozilla Web Thing API [16]. WOTS2E [17] proposes a search engine based on web crawling to use the semantic data. It provides a scalable and flexible approach for discovering web-connected devices using SPARQL. This system offers a RESTful API to support the creation of complex services by combining information from various web-based sources. The main goal of WOTS2E is to associate semantically rich and accessible information to real world things. In this sense, our approach is aimed at providing an easy mechanism to include and manage the semantic information related to the WoT resources.

5 Conclusions

This paper has proposed a discovery mechanism to support the management of WoT resources by integrating WoT applications through a search engine. The search process is, on the one hand, achieved by federated discovery services linked to propagate the queries and, on the other, managed by recommenders to filter and rank the WoT resources obtained as a result. We can conclude that our approach allows the (a) publication of the resources, (b) query of the available data and services, and (c) dynamic addition of new WoT directories.

Acknowledgments. This work has been funded by EU ERDF and Spanish MINECO under research projects CoSmart and FAME (ref. TIN2017-83964-R and RTI2018-093608-B-C33), and by regional projects (ref. CEIJ-C01.1 and CEIJ-C01.2) coordinated from UAL-UCA and funded by CEIMAR consortium.

References

1. Gravina, R., Palau, C.E., Manso, M., Liotta, A., Fortino, G. (eds.): Integration, Interconnection, and Interoperability of IoT Systems. IT. Springer, Cham (2018). https://doi.org/10.1007/978-3-319-61300-0
2. Kovatsch, M., Matsukura, R., Lagally, M., Kawaguchi, T., Toumura, K., Kajimoto, K.: Web of Things (WoT) Architecture, W3C Recommendation (2020)
3. Kaebisch, S., Kamiya, T., McCool, M., Charpenay, V., Kovatsch, M.: Web of Things (WoT) Thing Description, W3C Recommendation (2020)
4. Bröring, A., et al.: Enabling IoT ecosystems through platform interoperability. IEEE soft. **34**(1), 54–61 (2017)
5. Newcomer, E., Lomow, G.: Understanding SOA with Web Services. Addison-Wesley, Boston (2005)
6. Service Directory, Google Cloud. https://cloud.google.com/service-directory. Accessed 29 Apr 2020
7. Pahl, M., Liebald, S.: A modular distributed IoT service discovery. In: IFIP/IEEE Symposium on Integrated Network and Service Management (IM), Arlington, VA, USA, pp. 448–454. IEEE (2019)
8. Chan, N.N., Gaaloul, W., Tata, S.: A recommender system based on historical usage data for web service discovery. Serv. Oriented Comput. Appl. **6**(1), 51–63 (2012)
9. Memon, S., Jensen, J., Elbers, W., Neukirchen, H., Book, M., Riedel, M.: Towards federated service discovery and identity management in collaborative data and compute cloud infrastructures. J. Grid Comput. **16**(4), 663–681 (2018)
10. Rosenberg, F., Müller, M.B., Leitner, P., Michlmayr, A., Bouguettaya, A., Dustdar, S.: Metaheuristic optimization of large-scale QoS-aware service compositions. In: IEEE International Conference on Services Computing, Miami, FL, USA, pp. 97–104. IEEE (2010)
11. Tran, N.K., Sheng, Q.Z., Babar, M.A., Yao, L.: Searching the Web of Things: state of the art, challenges, and solutions. ACM Comput. Surv. **50**(4), 1–34 (2017)
12. Zhou, Y., De, S., Wang, W., Moessner, K.: Search techniques for the Web of Things: a taxonomy and survey. Sensors **16**(5), 600 (2016)
13. Sciullo, L., Aguzzi, C., Di Felice, M., Cinotti, T.S.: WoT store: enabling things and applications discovery for the W3C Web of Things. In: 16th IEEE Annual Consumer Communications & Networking Conference, Las Vegas, NV, USA, pp. 1–8. IEEE (2019)
14. Ostermaier, B., Römer, K., Mattern, F., Fahrmair, M., Kellerer, W.: A real-time search engine for the Web of Things. In: 2010 Internet of Things (IOT), Tokyo, Japan, pp. 1–8. IEEE (2010)
15. Younan, M., Khattab, S., Bahgat, R.: WoTSF: a framework for searching in the Web of Things. In: 10th International Conference on Informatics and Systems, Giza, Egypt, pp. 278–285. ACM (2016)
16. Web Thing API. https://iot.mozilla.org/wot/. Accessed 29 May 2020
17. Kamilaris, A., Yumusak, S., Ali, M.I.: WOTS2E: a search engine for a semantic Web of Things. In: 2016 IEEE 3rd World Forum on Internet of Things (WF-IoT), Reston, VA, USA, pp. 436–441. IEEE (2016)

Extending W3C Thing Description to Provide Support for Interactions of Things in Real-Time

Daniel Flores-Martin[✉][ID], Javier Berrocal[ID], José García-Alonso[ID],
and Juan M. Murillo[ID]

Universidad de Extremadura, Badajoz, Spain
{dfloresm,jberolm,jgaralo,juanmamu}@unex.es

Abstract. The continuous growth of the Web of Things allows us to find devices with different characteristics. This variety of devices favours the creation of heterogeneous intelligent environments that also makes interoperability between them difficult. This is why both the scientific community and consortiums such as the W3C are working on solutions to improve the interoperability. In this sense, the W3C has recently proposed W3C Thing Description standard that allows the modeling and description of smart things in order to improve the interoperability among them. However, the interoperability provided improves the interactions between the devices, but does not make it possible to define when these interactions should occur. This provides the standard with an extra level of interoperability, which is required to optimize interactions between situation-dependent devices. This work presents an extension of the W3C Thing Description to provide it with the ability to adapt the description and the interoperability of the devices to the situation at run-time. This allows devices to connect to each other being aware of the different situations they may be involved in to establish smarter and real-time communications.

Keywords: Web of Things · W3C thing description · Situations · Interoperability

1 Introduction

The relevance of the Internet of Things (IoT) increases as more and more Internet connected-devices are developed. From small household appliances to complex systems for the industry, the IoT market continues to grow unstoppable and will reach 31 billion of connected devices by 2020 and 75 billion devices by 2025 [9]. While IoT allows us to remotely monitor and control smart devices, the World Wide Web Consortium (W3C) Web of Things (WoT) integrates *Things* with the Web even more intimately; hence, making those devices more accessible for applications and humans [8].

© Springer Nature Switzerland AG 2020
I.-Y. Ko et al. (Eds.): ICWE 2020 Workshops, LNCS 12451, pp. 30–41, 2020.
https://doi.org/10.1007/978-3-030-65665-2_4

The smart environments usually integrate heterogeneous devices with different characteristics, where a high level of interoperability is required to make the environment smarter. However, the variety of different protocols and manufacturers that cause this heterogeneity gives rise to the problem of *vendor lock-in*, which causes users dependence on a specific manufacturer or platform. This is why the interoperability required in heterogeneous environments can be limited or can only be achieved by using devices from the same manufacturer or using the same communication protocols.

The interoperability between intelligent devices is one of the biggest challenges of WoT due to the great heterogeneity of devices and protocols [18]. Because of this, the scientific community is developing solutions that improve the interoperability between devices and give end-users the freedom to choose virtually any device regardless of manufacturer or communication protocols to be integrated into a smart environment [14,15]. In this sense, the W3C has developed the W3C Thing Description (W3C-TD) [12], which is presented as a solution to counteract fragmentation in the WoT. That is why a particularly remarkable benefit of this standard is that it applies to any WoT application domain. The W3C-TD facilitates the modeling of entities but does not contemplate the relationships between them or the situations in which they may be found. These situations arise from the grouping of entities that pursue a common objective. In this sense, the communication among entities is based on the exchange of information between the entities to discover the current and desired state of the situation. Therefore, in a smart environment the desired state in a situation is achieved by solving the objectives of the entities by adapting their behaviour in real-time. Although the W3C is an important step in the interoperability of devices, its capabilities can be increased to manage the different situations in which entities are involved. If this is not achieved, both the connections among devices and their behaviour will be more generic and can not be personalised.

In this paper, an extension of the W3C-TD to provide support for interactions in real-time is presented. This extension provides the W3C-TD with the ability to identify the objectives and the situation in which the entities are, as well as to define a description of them to identify which devices should be related and how to cover the needs detected in the situations in real-time. This encourages proactivity and collaboration between entities in real-time in a simple way.

The rest of the document is structured as follows. Section 2 describes the motivations of this work defining the situation concept and emphasizing its relevance. Next, in Sect. 3 the W3C-TD standard is detailed. Then, in Sect. 4 the W3C-TD is extended to model different situations in smart environments. The discussion about this work is shown in Sect. 5 while some related works are analysed in Sect. 6. Finally, some conclusions are detailed in Sect. 7.

2   Motivations

Traditionally, interactions among entities, whether people or smart devices, to trigger or automate actions have been performed manually. However, the latest trends express the need that these interactions should be conducted more automatically, encouraging proactivity among entities and achieving a more social environment [5]. Just as a device can make a change in the environment, such as adjusting the illumination, it can also aim to reduce its energy consumption. Also, a person may desire a level of illumination and also be able to reduce energy consumption by reducing the performance of a device or complementing it with another. These similar and complementary characteristics encourage the creation of social environments where proactivity among entities, allowing to discover the desired states in the environment and the actions that can be triggered to reach these states. On the one hand, the similar characteristics of the entities refer to the common objectives that two or more entities have regarding the environment. On the other hand, the complementary characteristics refer to those actions that can be taken to change the state of the environment. In this sense, from the proactive grouping of entities the *situation* arises.

A *situation* is a conceptual grouping of entities that pursues a common goal. In this way, for the objective of establishing pop and rock music of two people, a smart music player can establish these two types of music in an alternative way to solve the detected objectives. Also, in the case of a person who is driving to his/her work and desires a certain temperature for comfort, the air-conditioning device in the workplace can be turned on so that when the person arrives a more comfortable temperature is set for him/her. In addition, the collaboration can even be encouraged with other devices such as fans and electronic windows to accommodate the temperature, allowing for multi-interaction between different entities to solve a common goal. Therefore, the possibilities in which entities can be involved are practically infinite and, thanks to their similar and complementary characteristics, they provide numerous types of situations in which they must collaborate to achieve a common objective arising from the context in which they find themselves. Below, an example to motivate the problem throughout the paper is shown.

Let's imagine a smart house equipped with different smart devices such as light bulbs, air conditioner, switches, or music players, where currently several people live. The devices can establish relationships with each other according to the different situations in the house. Depending on the situation, specific lighting can be set; a certain type of music can be played, the temperature can be set, or an electronic device can be turned on or off. In addition, the contextual information must be taken into account such as the date, the time, the location or any other information that can be gathered. Also, the level of brightness can vary from one room in the house to another, from the music that is playing or the people near the bulb. This is due to each situation has assigned values or objectives that must be established for the people's state of comfort to be reached in the smart home. Therefore, to achieve the detected objectives the entities must model specific situations to act accordingly. This modeling allows entities to be aware of the situation they are in and be able to make the necessary relationships to establish the level of lighting, temperature, or type of music desired.

The importance of the situation modeling in smart environment is present within the community. In [20], a situation is presented as an important element within the context of the entities, and practically any contextual information can be used for the characterization of situations. Also, in [7], Gomez et al. analyse different environments to discover the requirements of situations related to several domains. This analysis is performed to detect the most appropriate communication solutions depending on the domain of action. Besides, in [19] situations are also considered as crucial elements to create proactive and adaptive web services. These works are a sample of the importance of modeling situations in intelligent environments. Although there is not a standard proposed for the situation modeling, the W3C has great potential for the development of standards, protocols and guidelines to ensure the growth of new technologies in the long term [3]. Entity modeling in WoT environments is the first step to model the situations these entities are in. The W3C-TD already achieves this entity modeling, making it a strong candidate to continue with the situation modeling.

Therefore, the W3C-TD extension proposed in this paper allows the situations modeling where the entities and their situations and objectives are recognizable to achieve a situational interoperability in real-time. The following section introduces the W3C-TD standard to show its possibilities.

3   W3C Thing Description

The W3C-TD [12] is presented as a solution to counteract fragmentation in the WoT, by defining the Things in the WoT in a standard way. In the W3C-TD, a *Thing* is defined as the abstraction of a physical or virtual entity that needs to be represented for WoT applications. This entity may be a device, a logical component of a device, a local hardware component or even a logical entity such as a location (e.g. a room or a building). In addition, the W3C-TD defines the specification of a pattern with which one can interact with the properties, actions or events of the *Thing*. The virtual representation of a *Thing* can be defined by the *Thing* itself, or hosted externally (e.g., in a repository) due to *Thing* constraints (e.g., legacy devices or lack of internal storage). Also, a *Thing* is serialized as JSON-LD (JSON for Linked-Data) and provides support for:

- Semantic metadata, based on a RDF (Resource Description Framework) data models. The use of semantic annotation facilitates the extension and integration of the *Thing* with external contexts.
- Communication, providing *Things'* protocol support, data exchange formats and bindings to an interaction resource.
- Security, where requirements for accessing to the resources of *Things* can be described.
- A functional description of the WoT interface of a *Thing*. The minimum vocabulary is defined that supports three different interaction patterns:
  - Properties, which provide readable and/or writable, static or dynamic data.

- Actions, which represent non-immediate changes or internal processes of a *Thing*.
- Events, which can raise notifications when certain conditions are met.

Although the W3C-TD is a W3C recommendation, there are currently works that are summarising its benefits [13,17], and also other works that are using it to build a more interoperable WoT [4], and even pursuing objectives similar to those of this work where effects, states and goals are identified [16]. The W3C-TD proposes an interesting solution to achieve better interoperability in the WoT. Since this solution does not contemplate the possible relationships between things, the relationship can be achieved for the recognition of situations in which different things can be involved by extending the standard. This would provide the W3C-TD with an additional level of interoperability and would be a further step towards achieving greater interoperability within the WoT.

Following the example given above, the W3C-TD allows us to describe the entities in the smart home to know their properties and status, to trigger actions such as turning on the light bulb or playing music, and even to listen to events. However, the relationship between these entities depends on the situation they are in as well as the contextual information. Therefore, additional information about the entities is required to interpret the situation in which they are located. To address this problem, the following section describes the proposed extension for the W3C-TD to model different situations and their objectives based on the information that each entity provides in an intelligent environment.

4   Situations Modeling in the W3C-TD

This extension consists of providing the W3C-TD standard [12] with the capacity to model objectives and situations. In the Fig. 1 it is shown the extension of the W3C-TD class diagram where two new sub-classes are included to model these aspects (green): *ObjectiveAffordance* and *SituationAffordance*.

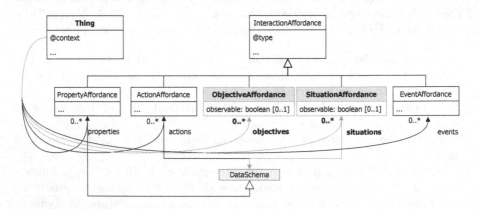

Fig. 1. Extended class diagram from W3C-TD (Color figure online)

These two new classes follow the patterns of the main classes already defined which are *PropertyAffordance*, *ActionAffordance* and *EventAffordance*. This is why the two sub-classes allow two new types of interactions within the description of the *Thing* or entity, both to model its objectives and the situations in case it has them. It may be the case that an entity does not have defined objectives, or that it does not have any situation stored. In Table 1 a brief description of these properties is shown.

Table 1. Thing properties included for objectives and situation modeling

Vocabulary term	Description	Assignment	Type
Objectives	Describes the objectives of the entity/thing. E.g. the luminosity level, type of music, desired temperature, bulb color, etc.	Optional	Map of ObjectiveAffordance
Situations	Describes the situation lived for the thing/entity in order to infer new objectives automatically	Optional	Map of SituationAffordance

In addition, the objectives and situations follow the same nomenclature as the original properties (*PropertyAffordance*). This is because they are still new terms or properties of the entity that can be created, consulted or removed by the entity to build its description (Table 2).

Table 2. ObjectiveAffordance and SituationAffordance definition

Vocabulary term	Description	Assignment	Type
Observable	A hint that indicates whether servients hosting the *Thing* and intermediaries should provide a protocol binding that supports the *observeproperty* operation for this property	Optional	Boolean

The two new sub-classes allow us to model objectives and situations from the metadata provided by the *DataSchema* element, as well as the main sub-classes of the W3C-TD. That is why in a *Thing* instance, the value assigned for objectives and situations is a map of *ObjectiveAffordance* and *SituationAffordance* instances, respectively. Following the W3C-TD standard, this means that all name-value pairs of a map must be serialized as members of the JSON object resulting from serializing the Map; the name of a pair must be serialized as a JSON string and the value of the pair, an instance of *ObjectiveAffordance* and *SituationAffordance*, must be serialized as a JSON object. In this sense, the objectives of the entity contain a map with the different goals it has. Each objective has the properties detailed in Table 3.

Table 3. Recommended properties for objectives modeling

Property	Description
Id	Objective ID
Name	Friendly name to be recognized easily in the environment
Value	The desired value for an environment status. E.g. the temperature (22%) or luminosity level (7 over 10) in a room
Properties	Contextual characteristics that define when the objectives occur such as the location, the time, the current weather or whatever other information that can be obtained from the environment

Likewise, situations also require certain information to be specified. The situations contain a map with the different situations that the entity has been going through, and that will be used to detect objectives automatically in the future. This information is detailed in Table 4.

Table 4. Recommended properties for situations modeling

Property	Description
Id	Situation ID
Name	Friendly name to be recognized easily in the environment
Properties	Contextual characteristics that define when the objectives occur such as the location, the time, the current weather or whatever other information that can be obtained from the environment
Objectives	A set with the objectives that have been identified along with the desired value and the entity to which it belongs
Things	The entities involved in the situation
Strategy	It indicates the actions conducted and the values to be established to solve the different objectives

An example to model an entity's objectives and situations is shown in Listing 1.1 and Listing 1.2, respectively. For the objectives, it is observed how the entity holds an objective called *temp*. In addition to its id and name, the objective provides the value that the entity wishes to be established in the environment to 22%. Also, the objective gives additional contextual information of the entity, such as the location or time when it occurs. The example of the situation is a little more complex, where a situation named *party-home* is detailed. Similarly, in addition to the id and the name, the situation also provides information about the contextual information. These properties are location, date, time, luminosity, and the weather. The situation also details which objectives were detected, such as the temperature that was desired by an entity as well as the type of music. Also, the situation collects information about other entities involved in that situation through its *id*, to establish a communication easily. Finally, the situation also specifies information about the strategy performed to cover the objectives.

In this case, the strategy conducted is to trigger the *temperature* action in the air conditioner to set the value to 23%, and also to invoke the action *music-type* in the media player to listen to pop music.

```
1  {
2      "@context": "...",
3      "properties": "...",
4      "actions": "...",
5      "events": "...",
6      ...
7      "objectives": {
8          "temp": {
9              "id": "temperature",
10             "name": "Home temperature",
11             "value": "22",
12             "properties": {
13                 "location": "39.4570601,-6.3835215",
14                 "time": "20:24:57 CET",
15                 ...
16             }
17         },
18         ...
19     },
20     "situations": "..."
21 }
```

Listing 1.1. Objetives description example

Once the description is specified, it must be shared. When an entity is detected in the environment its description is checked to obtain all the information. This information allows us to know if any of the situations stored is taking place. In this case, the entity establishes a connection with those entities with which it interacted previously to solve a known objective. If the situation is not recognized, it can be stored in the description of the entity to be used in the future. For this purpose, the data detailed above are stored and they serve to characterize the situation at present. The storage of this information is done by each entity but, in case of entities not having the capacity for storing information, the description can be stored in remote repositories or in a specific controller device installed in the environment to manage it. In the case of a person, this information is stored in his/her smartphone. In addition, this information could be modified in the life cycle of the entity and even deleted by the own entity to keep its description updated. This allows the entity to have the objectives and situations updated, maintaining the integrity of the data and to be located easily in the future. Also, to decide which entities should be connected between them, semantic reasoners and query languages such as SPARQL are used, taking advantage of the semantic capabilities of the W3C-TD to achieve more intelligent and real-time interoperability. As with storage, if the entity has the computing capacity to perform this process, it will do it itself. In this way, interoperability in an intelligent environment is enhanced to be dependent on the situation of the devices and to realize the relationships between them in an optimal way.

This extension achieves the modeling of objectives and situations of entities in smart environments. Therefore, these benefits provide support to the W3C-TD to improve interactions between entities and encourage their proactivity.

```
1  {
2    "@context": "...",
3    "properties": "...",
4    "actions": "...",
5    "events": "...",
6    "objectives": "...",
7    ...
8    "situations": {
9      "party-home": {
10       "id": "party-home",
11       "name": "Party at home for colleges",
12       "properties": {
13         "location": "39.4570601,-6.3835215",
14         "date": "2020-04-24",
15         "time": "21:30:00",
16         "luminosity": "7",
17         "weather": "sunny",
18         ...
19       },
20       "objectives": {
21         "type": "array",
22         "items": [
23           {
24             "thing": "id-Bob",
25             "objective": "id-temp",
26             "value": "23"
27           },
28           {
29             "thing": "id-Sara",
30             "objective": "id-music",
31             "value": "pop"
32           }, ...
33
34         ]
35       },
36       "things": {
37         "type": "array",
38         "items": [
39           "id-Bob","id-MediaPlayer","id-Sara",...,"id-
   AirConditioner"
40         ]
41       },
42       "strategy": {
43         "type": "array",
44         "items": [
45           {
46             "thing": "id-AirConditioner",
47             "action": "temperature",
48             "value": "23"
49           },
50           {
51             "thing": "id-MediaPlayer",
52             "action": "music-type",
53             "value": "pop"
54           }, ...
55
56         ]
57       }
58     }, ...
59
60   }
61 }
```

Listing 1.2. Situations description example

5   Discussion

Some properties have been proposed to represent objectives and situations that an entity goes through during its life cycle, by providing the relationships with other entities. This process is conducted in real-time to ensure that the connections established are optimal at any moment. These properties solve the problems mentioned to identify the elements of each situation, such as detecting other entities when the situation occurs, what are the objectives, or how to act on it.

We are aware that storing every situation in the life cycle of an entity is unfeasible, so this storage can be performed by filtering or grouping situations based on their characteristics. This would allow reducing the number of situations by sacrificing the accuracy of these to be detected within an environment. So, the the main limitations of this work are based on the amount of data to be stored, as well as its processing. Although this is done by the entities themselves, there may be entities that are not able to do this process due to their hardware limitations. In this case, this process must be performed by another entity or a device placed in the environment for that purpose.

6   Related Work

Different solutions are being conducted for specific situations in WoT scenarios. Bonte et al. present in [2] a platform called MASSIF: a data-driven platform for the semantic annotation of and reasoning on WoT data, allowing the integration of multiple modular reasoning services that can collaborate to facilitate complex decision-making processes. In addition, a situation-conscious intelligent logistics enterprise architecture (SSLEA) is designed in [11] that uses a WoT ecosystem to facilitate the discovery and handling of exceptions during the execution of transport processes. Its objective is to provide a better and faster response to exceptions that occur in the ecosystem. The situation management is also addressed in [21], where LAURA is proposed -Lean AUtomatic code generation for situation-aware and business-awaRe Applications-: a flexible, service-oriented and general open-source conceptual architecture designed to support the deployment of decoupled WoT applications. Also, the characterization of situations and people's preferences proposed in [10] follows similar parameters to this paper, by identifying the situation through different elements of the environment and also the objective of the situation. In addition, the authors of this paper have proposed different solutions for managing situations in real-time in WoT environments based on contextual information [1,6], where this paper is inspired.

These works are a sample of the efforts for situation recognition in smart environments. However, the use of a standard is not contemplated. The use of a standard adds value in the development of a software solution since that means to adopt a methodology that is widely accepted. That is why we consider that the extension of the W3C-TD picks up the benefits that the standard already holds and also provides the modeling of situations in real-time for the WoT.

7   Conclusions and Future Works

In this work, an extension of the W3C-TD has been proposed to model situations in WoT environments in real-time. Many smart devices in the WoT and their heterogeneity make it necessary to describe them to be easily identified in intelligent environments. The W3C-TD aims to make this description simple and user-friendly and can be easily interpreted by both humans and machines. However, other mechanisms are needed that are also capable of identifying the different situations in which the devices in that environment are found.

This extension makes it possible to use the information from the entities to identify the situation in which they find themselves and to be able to establish more intelligent connections between them to adapt their behaviour to the characteristics of the situation. In future works, we will validate this integration through the exchange of information between entities to discover situations based on their previously established description and to establish strategies for solving them. Also, the evaluation of this solution considers the cost, both in time and energy consumption, of the transfer of information between entities to discover the situations and resolve the detected objectives.

Acknowledgments. This work was supported by the Spanish Ministry of Science and Innovation through project RTI2018-094591-B-I00 (MCI/AEI/FEDER, UE) and FPU17/02251 grant, by 4IE+ project (0499-4IE-PLUS-4-E) funded by the Interreg V-A España-Portugal (POCTEP) 2014–2020 program, by the Department of Economy, Science and Digital Agenda of the Government of Extremadura (GR18112, IB18030), and by the European Regional Development Fund.

References

1. Berrocal, J., Garcia-Alonso, J., Canal, C., Murillo, J.M.: Situational-context: a unified view of everything involved at a particular situation. In: Bozzon, A., Cudre-Maroux, P., Pautasso, C. (eds.) ICWE 2016. LNCS, vol. 9671, pp. 476–483. Springer, Cham (2016). https://doi.org/10.1007/978-3-319-38791-8_34
2. Bonte, P., et al.: The MASSIF platform: a modular and semantic platform for the development of flexible IoT services. Knowl. Inf. Syst. **51**(1), 89–126 (2017)
3. Bopdesign, J.: The importance of W3C standards, June 2013. https://www.bopdesign.com/bop-blog/2013/06/the-importance-of-w3c-standards/. Accessed 20 Apr 2020
4. Ciortea, A., Boissier, O., Ricci, A.: Engineering world-wide multi-agent systems with hypermedia. In: Weyns, D., Mascardi, V., Ricci, A. (eds.) EMAS 2018. LNCS (LNAI), vol. 11375, pp. 285–301. Springer, Cham (2019). https://doi.org/10.1007/978-3-030-25693-7_15
5. Conti, M., Passarella, A.: The internet of people: a human and data-centric paradigm for the next generation Internet. Comput. Commun. **131**, 51–65 (2018)
6. Flores-Martin, D.: Meeting IoT users' preferences by emerging behavior at runtime. In: Braubach, L., et al. (eds.) ICSOC 2017. LNCS, vol. 10797, pp. 333–338. Springer, Cham (2018). https://doi.org/10.1007/978-3-319-91764-1_27

7. Gomez, C., Chessa, S., Fleury, A., Roussos, G., Preuveneers, D.: Internet of things for enabling smart environments: a technology-centric perspective. J. Ambient Intell. Smart Environ. **11**(1), 23–43 (2019)
8. Guinard, D., Trifa, V.: Building the Web of Things: with Examples in Node. js and Raspberry Pi. Manning Publications Co., Shelter Island (2016)
9. Horwitz, L.: The future of IoT miniguide: the burgeoning IoT market continues, July 2019. https://www.cisco.com/c/en/us/solutions/internet-of-things/future-of-iot.html. Accessed on 17 Mar 2020
10. Hussein, D., Han, S.N., Lee, G.M., Crespi, N., Bertin, E.: Towards a dynamic discovery of smart services in the social internet of things. Comput. Electric. Eng. **58**, 429–443 (2017)
11. Iacob, M.E., Charismadiptya, G., van Sinderen, M., Piest, J.P.S.: An architecture for situation-aware smart logistics. In: IEEE 23rd International Enterprise Distributed Object Computing Workshop (EDOCW), pp. 108–117. IEEE (2019)
12. Kaebisch, S., Kamiya, T., McCool, M., Charpenay, V.: Web of things (WoT) thing description. First Public Working Draft W3C (2017)
13. McCool, M., Reshetova, E.: Distributed security risks and opportunities in the W3C web of things. In: Workshop on Decentralized IoT Security and Standards (DISS) (2018)
14. Miori, V., Russo, D., Ferrucci, L.: Interoperability of home automation systems as a critical challenge for IoT. In: 4th International Conference on Computing, Communications and Security, ICCCS 2019. Institute of Electrical and Electronics Engineers Inc., October 2019. https://doi.org/10.1109/CCCS.2019.8888125
15. Noura, M., Atiquzzaman, M., Gaedke, M.: Interoperability in internet of things: taxonomies and open challenges. Mobile Netw. Appl. **24**(3), 796–809 (2019)
16. Noura, M., Gaedke, M.: Wotdl: Web of things description language for automatic composition. In: IEEE/WIC/ACM International Conference on Web Intelligence (WI), pp. 413–417. IEEE (2019)
17. Poggi, F., Rossi, D., Ciancarini, P.: Integrating semantic run-time models for adaptive software systems. J. Web Eng. **18**(1), 1–42 (2019)
18. Razzaque, M.A., Milojevic-Jevric, M., Palade, A., Clarke, S.: Middleware for internet of things: a survey. IEEE Internet Things J. **3**(1), 70–95 (2015)
19. Sekkal, N., Benslimane, S.M., Mrissa, M., Boudaa, B.: Combining proactive and reactive approaches in smart services for the web of things. In: Amine, A., Mouhoub, M., Ait Mohamed, O., Djebbar, B. (eds.) CIIA 2018. IAICT, vol. 522, pp. 509–520. Springer, Cham (2018). https://doi.org/10.1007/978-3-319-89743-1_44
20. Sezer, O.B., Dogdu, E., Ozbayoglu, A.M.: Context-aware computing, learning, and big data in internet of things: a survey. IEEE Internet Things J. **5**(1), 1–27 (2017)
21. Teixeira, S., et al.: Laura architecture: towards a simpler way of building situation-aware and business-aware IoT applications. J. Syst. Softw. **161**, 110494 (2020)

Second Semantics and the Web for Transport Workshop (Sem4Tra 2020)

Second Edition of the Semantics and the Web for Transport Workshop (Sem4Tra2020)

David Chaves-Fraga[1] (iD), Pieter Colpaert[2] (iD), Marco Comerio[3] (iD),
Mario Scrocca[1] (iD), and Mersedeh Sadeghi[2] (iD)

[1] Ontology Engineering Group, Universidad Politécnica de Madrid, Spain
[2] IDLab – imec, Ghent University, Belgium
[3] Cefriel – Dipartimento di Elettronica, Informazione e Bioingegneria,
Politecnico di Milano, Italy

Abstract. Mobility-as-a-Service (MaaS) integrates different transport services into a single mobility service. The goal is to provide a traveler with all the services needed for door-to-door travel under a single payment whilst integrating disparate modes of mobility (public transport, car- or bike-sharing, taxi/car rental, or a combination thereof) under one travel experience. After years of conceptualization and strategizing, MaaS is becoming a reality rather than a future goal. However, many challenges remain unanswered. The development of multimodal travel information, planning and booking services, and interoperability between business applications is currently limited due to the fragmentation and incompatibility of interchange formats and protocols both within and across transport sectors. The foundation of the Semantic Web and technologies such as RDF and Linked Data foster utilization and application of the semantics of terms in a decentralized fashion on Web scale. Given the decentralized nature of MaaS, this workshop targets researchers and practitioners who are contributing to the transformation of the transportation sector by proposing new Semantic and Web API-based solutions to achieve the MaaS objectives. The workshop is an opportunity to disseminate and discuss use cases and studies showing the application of Semantic and Web technologies in the Transport domain to tackle the abovementioned challenges.

1 The Workshop

This year's workshop was in combination with WOT4H and the KDWEB workshops and was held virtually, as the COVID-19 pandemic prevented us from traveling. A long paper, a short paper, and a demo paper were presented.

2 Program Committee

We would like to thank our dedicated Program Committee:

Alessio Carenini   Cefriel
Edna Ruckhaus   Universidad Politécnica de Madrid

Irene Celino	Cefriel
Julián Rojas	imec – IDLab UGent
Letizia Tanca	Politecnico di Milano
Marlene Gonçalves	Universidad Simón Bolívar
Matteo Giovanni Rossi	Politecnico di Milano
Oscar Corcho	Universidad Politécnica de Madrid
Riccardo Santoro	Ferrovie dello Stato Italiane
Ruben Taelman	imec – IDLab UGent

Interactive Route Personalization Using Regions of Interest

Harm Delva[1]([✉]), Annelien Smets[2], Pieter Colpaert[1], Pieter Ballon[2],
and Ruben Verborgh[1]

[1] IDLab, Department of Electronics and Information Systems,
Ghent University – Imec, Ghent, Belgium
harm.delva@gmail.com, harm.delva@ugent.be
[2] imec-SMIT, Vrije Universiteit Brussel, Etterbeek, Belgium

Abstract. There is an abundance of services and applications that find
the most efficient route between two places, people are not always interested in efficiency; sometimes we just want a pleasant route. Such routes
are subjective though, and may depend on contextual factors that route
planners are oblivious to. One possible solution is to automatically learn
what a user wants, but this requires behavioral data, leading to a cold
start problem. An alternative approach is to let the user express their
desires explicitly, effectively helping them create the most pleasant route
themselves. In this paper we provide a proof of concept of a client-side
route planner that does exactly that. We aggregated the Point of Interest information from OpenStreetMap into Regions of Interest, and published the results on the Web. These regions are described semantically,
enabling the route planner to align the user's input to what is known
about their environment. Planning a 3 km long pedestrian route through
a city center takes 5 s, but subsequent adjustments to the route require
less than a second to compute. These execution times imply that our
approach is feasible, although further optimizations are needed to bring
this to the general public.

Keywords: Linked open data · Point of Interest · Route planning ·
OpenStreetMap

1 Introduction

Route planning applications have become so common that many, such as Google
Maps, have almost become household names. The majority of these applications
focus on generating the most efficient route, even though people are not always
interested in efficiency. Some people may want to enjoy the first days of good
weather by making a small detour through a local park, others may want to
avoid the same park because of allergies. There are also pragmatic reasons for
wanting to avoid certain places: shopping streets can get overcrowded on Satur-
day afternoons, and parks may also get overcrowded – which can be a problem
during pandemics for instance.

© Springer Nature Switzerland AG 2020
I.-Y. Ko et al. (Eds.): ICWE 2020 Workshops, LNCS 12451, pp. 47–52, 2020.
https://doi.org/10.1007/978-3-030-65665-2_5

The list of examples goes on, which is exactly the problem we address in this paper: the ideal route depends on personal preference and contextual factors, many of which are subjective and change over time. Instead of trying to predict what a user wants, we propose to let them specify their preferences explicitly through an interactive application.

2   Related Work

The subjective value of routes is not a new scientific subject; philosophers in 1955 even coined the term *psychogeography* for the study of how people experience their environment [5], and by extension, how they experience navigating through it. Research in this field addressed questions such as how people perceive their commute to work [1] or how they value their time on the bus [7]. Today, the planning of personalized routes remains an open research question, with some researchers claiming that "insufficient criteria modeling for a personalized system" is one of the major difficulties [9], while others note that the innate flexibility of such route planners forms a computational problem [6].

One notable work in this field is aptly named "The Shortest Route to Happiness" [11], where the authors used quantitative measures of how people perceive different locations to recommend emotionally pleasing routes to their destination. Their user study revealed two important lessons for further research: on one hand, it confirms that users can indeed appreciate pleasant routes over efficient routes. However, they nuanced this by adding that context plays an important role. For instance, the pleasantness of a location changes throughout the day, and not everyone appreciates crowded shopping streets. The authors suggested that future work could focus on incorporating these preferences through personalizaton.

The latter is, however, a delicate operation. Several scholars have raised concerns about algorithmic personalization based on users' historic preferences. They argue that this kind of personalization might result in a decrease of exposure diversity, a problem that is known as the so-called filter bubble [3,8,10]. In an urban environment, this results in people being exposed to different parts of the city [13], which deteriorates the opportunities that arise in diverse urban contexts and could in turn reinforce societal stereotypes. To overcome this, scholars have suggested to increase the incompleteness of the digital information environment [2]. They argue that this invites users to explore more actively and thus provides the opportunity to escape their bubble.

3   Method

We propose to drop the assumption that user preferences have to be predicted, or learned, and instead develop a proof of concept application that asks the user for their preferences explicitly. Users have the ability to personalize their own route, which is not only a solution to the data availability problem, it also puts the user back in control of the results they see.

Fig. 1. Visualized on the right are the clusters that are found by running the clustering algorithm on the cells of entities that have a `shop` tag, visualized on the left. If a sufficient amount of cells are sufficiently close to each other, they are placed in the same cluster. This is a variation of the well-known DBSCAN algorithm, and choosing appropriate values for these parameters can be challenging. However, it is made easier because we are working on a discrete input space. If we only consider directly adjacent cells as neighboring, there can be at most 6 cells in a cell's neighborhood, and by running the algorithm for each of these values we obtain a set of clusters of increasing strictness. We have found good results by setting the maximum distance to 2, in which case there are at 18 possible neighboring cells, and we add a padding layer of 1 cell around every found region.

At the core of our approach lie *Regions of Interest*, which contain several *Points of Interest* (POIs) such as shops, public parks, restaurants, etc. These regions are obtained by placing the publicly available POI data from the OpenStreetMap project[1] of a given type (e.g., all shops) onto a discrete grid[2], and clustering the grid cells using a variation of DBSCAN. The discrete grid forms a unified representation for all locations, regardless of whether they are described as simple points or as multi-polygons, while a notion of density is retained by performing the clustering with increasingly strict parameters, as illustrated by Fig. 1. Every region is then semantically described, as in Listing 5.1, and the results are published through a Linked Data Fragments interface, similar to our existing Routable Tiles dataset [4].

```
1  [
2      {
3          "@type": "owl:Restriction",
4          "owl:onClass": "osm:Entity",
5          "owl:onProperty": "osm:hasTag",
6          "owl:someValuesFrom": [
7              "taginfo:shop=bicycle",
8              "taginfo:shop=hardware",
9              ...
10         ],
11         "@id": "_:CommercialEntity"
12     },
```

---

[1] Available as Linked Data Fragments, e.g. at https://opoi.org/14/8411/5485/.
[2] Using the H3 spatial index, see https://h3geo.org/.

```
13    {
14      "@id": "_:fuzzy_subject",
15      "rdfs:subPropertyOf": "dct:subject",
16      "truth:degree": 0.2222222
17    },
18    {
19      "geo:asWKT": "POLYGON ((3.0016827 51.2498880, 3.0018188
   ↪ 51.2496799, ...",
20      "_:fuzzy_subject": "_:CommercialEntity"
21    }
22  ]
```

Listing 5.1. JSON-LD representation of a single Region of Interest. Each region is described using terms from the GeoSPARQL vocabulary, and a `subject` property from dcterms refers to a description of the region's contents. These descriptions use OWL restriction classes to group similar kinds of POIs together. To model the specificity of different regions, we approximate the semantics of fuzzy sets by adding a self-defined `truth:degree` value to the `subject` properties, using the clustering strictness as a proxy for the membership value.

4   Demonstrator

A live version of the demonstrator is available at https://hdelva.be/sem4tra2020/demo.html, or through the HTML version of this paper at https://hdelva.be/articles/regions-of-interest-demo/. The demo works on all devices with a modern web browser, including mobile devices (in landscape mode), and computing a route for the default scenario takes roughly 5 s with subsequent adjustments taking less than a second.

Figure 2 contains a screenshot of the application, as well as a description of how it works. We let users provide their current preferences explicitly, which are then cross-referenced with a set of Regions of Interest to add additional weights to a road network, and Dijkstra's algorithm is used to perform the route planning itself. Although we only support pedestrian routing for the moment, the same principles can be applied to other modes of transport by constructing the base road network graph accordingly.

5   Discussion

As mentioned in Listing 5.1, our route planner only has a limited view of reality. It has a vague idea of where the shops are, but not which shops exactly, or how many. This information could be added through an additional data source, however the imprecise aggregated data has some interesting implications. The obvious one is that using aggregated data is less resource intensive; there is less data to process, and the processing itself is easier. One could start from the raw data, but this would add more workload to the client, and as noted in Sect. 2, personalized route planners are already computationally intensive.

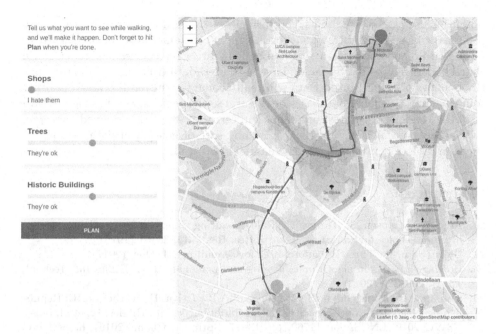

Fig. 2. A screenshot of the demonstrator calculating a route from the historic center of the city of Ghent to the train station, roughly 3 km apart. The different kinds of Regions of Interest are visualized on the map: green indicates nature, blue indicates shops, and orange-red indicates historic buildings. The red route shows the most efficient route, the blue route incorporates the user's preferences. Note that the main shopping streets are just to the south of the historic center, and that the personalized route circumvents them entirely, while still presenting a reasonably short route. (Color figure online)

Working entirely with intentionally imprecise data can also be a pragmatic solution to working around data quality issues. For example, it does not matter if the base data contains 20 out of 50 restaurants on a single street – it is a street with many restaurants. Clients are also shielded from the data model of the raw data, which means that even non-semantic data sources can be used, assuming some mapping happens during the aggregation.

The incompleteness of the results should also cause users to more actively explore their environment by presenting less complete information. Ultimately, this apparent loss of user experience should result in unexpected discoveries, users might be presented with serendipitous discoveries that are known to increase overall user satisfaction [12].

6   Conclusion

We have built a publicly available application that plans a pedestrian route from the historic center of Ghent to the train station, using aggregated Point of Interest data from the OpenStreetMap project. This application is just one potential use-case of the underlying principles though, and it hopefully it will serve as a basis for future work. For instance, the same data can be reused to build a different application that builds itineraries for tourists, or to visualize characteristics of a city. So far we have only used data from a single source, but the benefits of using Linked Data will really come to fruition if data from other sources, such as official databases of cultural heritage sites, is added as well. In fact, the Regions of Interest are defined in terms of externally defined concepts, so that anyone can generate them from any sort of geospatial data, as long as the source data can be described semantically as well.

References

1. Algers, S., Hansen, S., Tegner, G.: Role of waiting time, comfort, and convenience in modal choice for work trip. Transp. Res. Rec. **534**, 38–51 (1975)
2. Björneborn, L.: Three key affordances for serendipity. J. Doc. (2017)
3. Bozdag, E.: Bias in algorithmic filtering and personalization. Ethics Inf. Technol. **15**(3), 209–227 (2013)
4. Colpaert, P., Abelshausen, B., Meléndez, J.A.R., Delva, H., Verborgh, R.: Republishing OpenStreetMap's roads as linked routable tiles. In: Hitzler, P., et al. (eds.) ESWC 2019. LNCS, vol. 11762, pp. 13–17. Springer, Cham (2019). https://doi.org/10.1007/978-3-030-32327-1_3
5. Debord, G.: Introduction to a Critique of Urban Geography. Praxis (e) press (2008)
6. Funke, S., Storandt, S.: Personalized route planning in road networks. In: Proceedings of the 23rd SIGSPATIAL International Conference on Advances in Geographic Information Systems, pp. 1–10 (2015)
7. Horowitz, A.J.: Subjective value of time in bus transit travel. Transportation **10**(2), 149–164 (1981)
8. Jiang, R., Chiappa, S., Lattimore, T., György, A., Kohli, P.: Degenerate feedback loops in recommender systems. In: Proceedings of the 2019 AAAI/ACM Conference on AI, Ethics, and Society, pp. 383–390 (2019)
9. Niaraki, A.S., Kim, K.: Ontology based personalized route planning system using a multi-criteria decision making approach. Expert Syst. Appl. **36**(2), 2250–2259 (2009)
10. Pariser, E.: The Filter Bubble: How the New Personalized Web is Changing What We Read and How We Think. Penguin, Westminster (2011)
11. Quercia, D., Schifanella, R., Aiello, L.M.: The shortest path to happiness: recommending beautiful, quiet, and happy routes in the city. In: Proceedings of the 25th ACM conference on Hypertext and Social Media, pp. 116–125 (2014)
12. Reviglio, U.: Serendipity as an emerging design principle of the infosphere: challenges and opportunities. Ethics Inf. Technol. **21**(2), 151–166 (2019). https://doi.org/10.1007/s10676-018-9496-y
13. Smets, A., Montero, E., Ballon, P.: Does the bubble go beyond? In: Proceedings of The 1st Workshop on the Impact of Recommender Systems with ACM RecSys 2019 (2019)

Velopark: A Linked Open Data Platform for Bicycle Parkings

Julián Andrés Rojas[1]([✉])(iD), Pieter Morlion[2], Han Tambuyzer[3], Wout Baert[4], Pieter Colpaert[1](iD), and Ruben Verborgh[1](iD)

[1] IDLab, Department of Electronics and Information Systems,
Ghent University – imec, Ghent, Belgium
julianandres.rojasmelendez@ugent.be
[2] More-Lion, Smart Mobility Office, Gentbrugge, Belgium
[3] Nazka Mapps, Leuven, Belgium
[4] Fietsberaad Vlaanderen, Brussels, Belgium

Abstract. Cycling as a mean of urban transportation is positively correlated with cleaner, healthier and happier cities. By providing more infrastructure, such as secure parking facilities, cities aim on attracting more cyclists. However, authoritative information about parking facilities is heavily decentralized and heterogeneous, which makes secure parking facilities harder to be discovered by cyclists. Can an open dataset about bike parkings be managed decentrally? In this paper, we present the results of the Velopark project, carried out in Belgium by different actors that include local public authorities, public transport operators and pro-cycling organizations. During the project execution we (i) introduced the Open Velopark Vocabulary as a common semantic data model; and (ii) implemented the Velopark platform, an open data publishing environment for both static and live authoritative parking data. So far, 1599 parking facilities were published through the Velopark platform, 31 different Belgian municipalities and 4 parking related organizations use the platform to describe, publish and manage their parking facilities. A common data publishing environment supports organizations for providing access to their information, while guaranteeing data reliability for cyclists. In future work we will further extend our data model to cover other kinds of infrastructure and bicycle-related services.

Keywords: Bicycle parking · Linked open data · Urban transport · Domain model · RDF

1 Introduction

Bicycles have played a main role in the urban transportation evolution of the last decade [8]. Motivated by its positive side-effects (e.g., on traffic congestion, CO2 emissions and public health), public authorities around the world implement strategies that promote cycling as a main mode of transportation [1,15].

Available online at https://julianrojas.org/papers/sem4tra2020-paper.

© Springer Nature Switzerland AG 2020
I.-Y. Ko et al. (Eds.): ICWE 2020 Workshops, LNCS 12451, pp. 53–64, 2020.
https://doi.org/10.1007/978-3-030-65665-2_6

Countries such as Denmark, Germany and The Netherlands, stand among the most successful in this regard [11], due to effective pro-cycling policies combined with adequate infrastructure provision (e.g., parking facilities) [2,6].

Sufficient infrastructure coverage and capacity is necessary to increase bicycle usage, but infrastructure alone is not enough. Effective information channels that let cyclists know where and how to access and use such infrastructure are also a necessity. Lack of clear communication may lead to increased inappropriate (sometimes illegal) street parking and higher bicycle theft levels. These are already major issues in the aforementioned countries, ultimately having negative effects on cycling promotion [9,14].

Nowadays cyclists struggle to find reliable and useful information. Authoritative data about bicycle-related infrastructure such as parkings, is usually managed by multiple organizations that either own or operate these facilities. The Web is typically the preferred medium used by these organizations to make information available to the public via their websites. However, having to visit several websites is impractical to find the desired information, e.g., to know where to securely park a bike or if there is enough room to do so in a particular location.

Applications that facilitate information access are difficult to build due to highly heterogeneous or unavailable data. Providing users with all mobility-related information they need, is one of the goals behind MaaS (Mobility as a Service)[1] solutions. Building MaaS applications requires data to be available in machine-readable formats, which is frequently not the case for bicycle-related infrastructure. Acknowledging this gap and motivated by Open Data initiatives, some bicycle infrastructure managers publish their data using machine-readable formats through *ad-hoc* Web APIs. Although they fulfill their purpose of making data available, developers still struggle on reusing the data due to the high heterogeneity found across APIs in terms of data structure and information detail.

In this paper we present the results of the Velopark project[2]. This project was carried out in Belgium with the support of local governments, public transport operators and pro-cycling organizations. The main results of the project are (i) a semantic data model, namely the Open Velopark Vocabulary[3] to effectively describe bicycle parking facilities; (ii) the implementation of a data publishing platform that supports organizations with limited resources to manage and self-publish their data, while fostering interoperability of bicycle parking data; and (iii) an Open Data charter[4] signed by the cities of Antwerp, Ghent, Leuven, Pelt and other organizations, expressing a commitment to provide timely and high quality information about their bicycle parkings as interoperable Open Data to stimulate daily bicycle use. At the time of writing, 31 Belgian municipalities and 4 bicycle parking related organizations actively engaged into the Velopark platform, publishing 1599 bicycle parking facilities.

---

[1] https://maas-alliance.eu/homepage/what-is-maas/.
[2] https://www.velopark.be/en/about.
[3] https://velopark.ilabt.imec.be/openvelopark/vocabulary.
[4] https://www.velopark.be/charte-velopark-en.pdf.

The rest of this paper is organized as follows: Sect. 2 presents an overview of related work regarding data models and approaches for Open Data publishing on the Web. Section 3 describes the Open Velopark vocabulary. Section 4 presents the reference architecture of the Velopark platform. Finally in Sect. 5, we present our conclusions and vision for future work.

2   Related Work

In this section we present an overview of related data models that up to different degrees, describe bicycle-related infrastructure. We also describe different approaches that are currently followed to publish bicycle-related information as Open Data.

2.1   Modeling Bicycle Infrastructure Data

Providing cyclists with useful information about related infrastructure such as parkings, requires models able to capture and describe all their relevant characteristics and features. Definitions of entities and properties related to cycling infrastructure can be found in general purpose vocabularies like Schema.org[5]. For example `schema:ParkingFacility` or `schema:openingHours` represent two concepts directly related to the modeling bicycle parkings. However, Schema.org does not consider many domain-specific aspects, needed for giving detailed and useful information to cyclists. This occurs because Schema.org is meant to provide descriptions for a core of common topics, relying on extensions to cover more in-depth topic's details [5].

This creators of MobiVoc[6] followed the same rationale. MobiVoc defines a vocabulary for mobility-related concepts that extends Schema.org classes by establishing *subclass* relations with Schema.org classes. Such relations are established by means of the `rdfs:subClassOf` predicate. Even though MobiVoc specializes on mobility and further defines domain related concepts, it still lacks coverage for cyclic infrastructure specific entities. For example, it does not give definitions for parking security features, which often are important criteria for cyclist looking for parking places.

Other related work includes the Parking Ontology[7], the General Bikeshare Feed Specification (GBFS)[8] and the Mobility Data Specification (MDS)[9]. The Parking Ontology focuses on describing car parking areas and does not consider bicycle-related domain knowledge. GBFS defines a JSON-based specification for real-time and read-only data about status of bike sharing stations. MDS defines a set of APIs to facilitate information exchange between public authorities and dockless mobility service providers (e.g., e-scooters, mopeds, bicycles).

---

[5] https://schema.org.

[6] http://schema.mobivoc.org/.

[7] http://ontology.eil.utoronto.ca/icity/Parking/.

[8] https://github.com/NABSA/gbfs.

[9] https://github.com/openmobilityfoundation/mobility-data-specification.

Both GBFS and MDS are mostly focused on describing operational aspects of mobility services and lack formal semantics on their data models.

2.2   Bicycle Infrastructure as Open Data

Open and machine-readable data is fundamental for the creation of applications that provide useful and reliable information to cyclists. Infrastructure managers commonly publish their data in the form of data dumps or via HTTP APIs. For instance, the data portal of the city of Ghent, Belgium publishes their bicycle parking data[10] using both approaches.

OpenStreetMap (OSM) can also be considered as an open data source for bicycle infrastructure information [4]. It also provides data dumps and can be queried via the Overpass API[11]. Given their high server cost, open HTTP APIs often impose request limits (as is the case for Ghent and Overpass endpoints) or expect to handle simple queries only [10]. Data dumps on the other hand, can be seen as a mirror of the original data source and are outdated since the moment of their creation, which becomes an issue, specially when publishing live data [12].

Another popular alternative, motivated by SEO (Search Engine Optimization) guidelines is the embedding of structured data into HTML using Schema.org as a data model, and JSON-LD or RDFa as serialization formats. This helps search engines to better classify and index websites, but it is hard to reuse by applications due to discoverability and even legal issues when scraping websites.

3   Open Velopark Vocabulary

Motivated by the need of having a common data model capable of capturing all the complexity inherent to bicycle parkings, we created the Open Velopark Vocabulary (OVV)[12]. We incorporated the input of several bicycle parking managers, which includes public authorities, public transport operators and pro-cycling organizations, all having the goal of bringing reliable and useful information to bicycle users. For the vocabulary creation we followed the guidelines established by the Best Practices for publishing Linked Data[13] document, emphasizing on reusing standard and existing vocabularies.

The core of OVV is based on MobiVoc, which is in its turn based on the Schema.org data model. OVV thus extends both MobiVoc and Schema.org to define a set of concepts and properties that are not originally considered by these vocabularies and are deemed important for providing useful information for cyclists (see Fig. 1). The main focus of OVV extensions lies in providing

---

[10] https://data.stad.gent/explore/dataset/real-time-bezettingen-fietsenstallingen-gent/information/.

[11] https://wiki.openstreetmap.org/wiki/Overpass_API.

[12] https://velopark.ilabt.imec.be/openvelopark/vocabulary.

[13] https://www.w3.org/TR/ld-bp/.

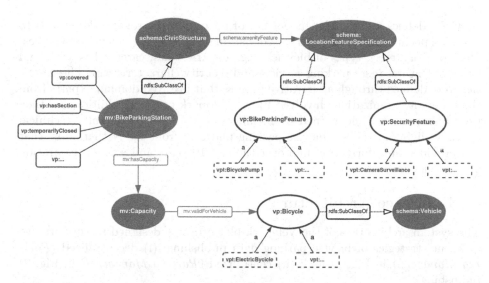

Fig. 1. Overview of OVV that shows how it relates and extends concepts from Schema.org and MobiVoc.

Table 1. OVV avoids to redefine existing concepts and adds domain-specific entities and properties.

Name	Type	Extends
Bicycle	Class	schema:Vehicle
Bike Parking Feature	Class	schema:LocationFeatureSpecification
Securiity Feature	Class	schema:LocationFeatureSpecification
has section	Object Property	mv:BicycleParkingStation
has counting system	Data Property	mv:Capacity
covered	Data Property	mv:BicycleParkingStation
final closing date	Data Property	mv:BicycleParkingStation
intended audience	Data Property	mv:BicycleParkingStation
minimum parking duration	Data Property	mv:BicycleParkingStation
opening hours extra information	Data Property	mv:BicycleParkingStation
post removal action	Data Property	mv:BicycleParkingStation
removal conditions	Data Property	mv:BicycleParkingStation
restrictions	Data Property	mv:BicycleParkingStation
initial opening date	Data Property	mv:BicycleParkingStation
temporarily closed	Data Property	mv:BicycleParkingStation

definitions for bicycle parking associated services and features and more detailed descriptions of operational and physical properties of bicycle parking facilities (see Table 1).

OVV defines a core-independent list of terms[14] that provides definitions to domain-specific entities such as types of parking facilities (e.g., bicycle stand, resident parking, etc.), types of bicycles (e.g., electric bikes, cargo bikes, etc.) and types of features (e.g., parking services and security characteristics). These entities were defined through an iterative process that involved domain experts from the different organizations involved in the Velopark project. Additionally, they were also reviewed and refined by members of the VeiligStallen.nl[15] technical team. VeiligStallen.nl is a bicycle parking platform from the Netherlands, that has provided an information hub over the last 10 years and was an inspiration of the Velopark initiative.

4   Reference Architecture

The system architecture of the Velopark platform was designed to support two different strategies of bicycle parking data publishing: (i) decentralized (*Parking Manager A* in Fig. 2) and; (ii) centralized (*Parking Manager B* in Fig. 2) publishing.

The first strategy enables a decentralized data management process. Bicycle Parking Managers (BPMs) are able to use Velopark's *Snippet Generator* tool to describe their facilities following the OVV data model, and then opt for publish the resulting data on their own servers. Every BPM decides on how to publish the data, requiring only to make the parking facility URIs dereferenceable and set the appropriate HTTP headers for enabling CORS (Cross-Domain Resource Sharing). Some alternatives to publish the data are (i) embedding JSON-LD snippets in BPMs website HTML; (ii) using HTTP content-negotiation to give both machine- and human-oriented views of the data; or (iii) serving the data as plain RDF files. Figure 2 represents scenario *iii* through *Parking Manager A*.

The centralized strategy focuses on supporting organizations with limited resources to self-host and manage the data about their parking facilities. These organizations can also use Velopark's *Snippet Generator* tool to create a data description of their facilities using the OVV model, but unlike the decentralized strategy, data is published and maintained on Velopark servers as plain RDF (JSON-LD) files. *Parking Manager B* is an example of this scenario in Fig. 2.

Regardless of the data publishing strategy (either centralized or decentralized), the Velopark platform remains a central and authoritative data entry point. This is achieved by maintaining a DCAT[16] catalog linking to all available parking facility URIs, which are in turn dereferenceable and contain the parkings data.

4.1   Snippet Generator

This Web application (available at https://admin.velopark.be) is designed to enable BPMs describing their parking facilities following the OVV model.

---

[14] https://velopark.ilabt.imec.be/openvelopark/terms#.
[15] https://www.veiligstallen.nl/.
[16] https://www.w3.org/TR/vocab-dcat-2/.

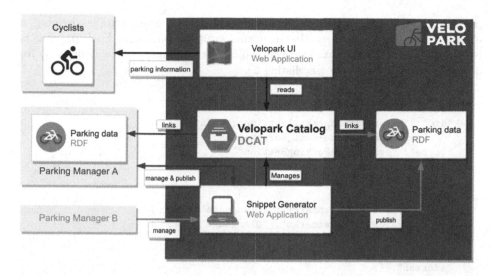

Fig. 2. Velopark's DCAT catalog allows applications to get a complete and reliable list of all parking facilities, enabling access to the data directly from their authoritative sources.

Additionally, BPMs have the possibility to manage their facilities by updating them and deciding if they are referenced in Velopark's data catalog. BPMs publishing parking data on Velopark's platform are required to follow these steps:

1. *Registration:* BPMs can be either public authorities representing a certain municipality or company representatives. They first request access to the platform which is granted by Fietsberaad Vlaanderen.
2. *Parking Description:* Once registered, BPMs can describe their facilities by entering the data in a wizard-based form, which ensures that all basic and required properties are entered.
3. *Data Publishing:* When the description of a parking facility has been completed, BPMs have the option to either self-host the data or rely on Velopark's servers to host it. In case self-hosting is chosen, BPMs need to provide the URL where the parking data will be made available. The application will generate a JSON-LD snippet (see Listing 1) containing all the parking data that has to be published under the chosen URL. Otherwise, the application will generate a URI (belonging to Velopark's domain) for the parking facility and will proceed to make the data available there.

4.2 Velopark DCAT Catalog

Velopark's data catalog is the result of the work done by BPMs on describing their parking facilities. It references all the parkings that have been approved by the BPMs to be made public, regardless of where the data is hosted (either on BPM or Velopark servers), bridging both centralized and decentralized data publishing strategies. The catalog follows the DCAT specification, defining a unique dcat:Catalog entity that contains multiple parkings. Each parking is represented as a dcat:Distribution, which data can accessed as defined by its dcat:accessURL property (see listing 2).

```
{
    "@context": { ... },
    "@id": "https://velopark.ilabt.imec.be/data/
        De-Fietsambassade-Gent_Korenmarkt",
    "@type": "mv:BicycleParkingStation",
    "dateModified": "2020-02-10T22:20:45.814Z",
    "identifier": "Korenmarkt",
    "name": [
        { "@value": "Korenmarkt", "@language": "nl" },
        { "@value": "Korenmarkt", "@language": "en" }
    ],
    "temporarilyClosed": false,
    "address": {
        "@type": "schema:PostalAddress",
        "postalCode": "9000",
        "streetAddress": "Pakhuisstraat",
        "country": "Belgium"
    }
    ...
}
```

Listing 1: JSON-LD description extract of a parking facility using the OVV data model. The data file can be dereferenced at the URL defined by the '@id' property of the JSON-LD data.

4.3   Velopark User Interface

This is a Web application[17] (see Fig. 3) targeted at cyclists and built by the Velopark team. It presents a map-based view containing all the available parking facilities of a certain region. It also creates human-oriented visualizations on top of parkings data, showing all the parking characteristics. Cyclists can filter the facilities by their properties such as features, services and physical characteristics. This application stands as an example of how Velopark's data can be discovered (via the catalog) and be directly consumed from their sources.

Another important feature of this application is the possibility for cyclists to provide feedback. If something is incorrect on the data of a particular parking facility or if some parkings are missing, cyclists can report this through the application. These reports will reach the corresponding public authority representatives responsible for the parking or the municipality mentioned in the report, which in turn can proceed to update the data where necessary.

---

[17] https://velopark.be.

```
{
    "@context": { ... },
    "@id": "http://velopark.ilabt.imec.be/data/catalog",
    "@type": "dcat:Catalog",
    "dcat:dataset": {
        "@type": "dcat:Dataset",
        "dcat:distribution": [
            {
                "@type": "dcat:Distribution",
                "dcat:accessURL": [
                  "https://velopark.ilabt.imec.be/data/Cyclopark_AL01"
                ],
                "dcat:mediaType": "application/ld+json",
                "dct:issued": "2020-02-04T17:12:27.035Z",
                "dct:modified": "2020-02-04T17:12:27.035Z"
            },
            ...
        ]
    }
}
```

Listing 2: The catalog is updated via the *Snippet Generator*, immediately reflecting any changes made by the BPMs, which constitutes a reliable source of data for cyclists and third-party applications.

4.4   Handling Live Data

One of the most important aspects for cyclists is to be informed about the live occupancy of a certain parking facility. Unfortunately these particular type of data is unavailable for most facilities. In the case of Velopark's BPMs, only three BPMs had an available API where this data could be found: the city of Ghent (for 2 parkings), Parko (for 1 parking in Kortrijk) and Blue-Bike (for 1 parking in Vilvoorde). We took the data available on these APIs and republished it using the OVV data model. The process to republish the live data is as follows:

1. *Data Modeling:* OVV already considers a class for representing live capacity values. The mv:RealTimeCapacity class defined by MobiVoc has precisely this purpose, which we reused.
2. *Linked Data Generation:* Since the original data comes through *ad-hoc* APIs that lack formal semantic definitions, we used RML (RDF Mapping Language) [3] to define the rules that describe how the data of each API should be annotated to follow the OVV data model. We created these mappings using the YARRRML [7] syntax.
3. *Live Data Publishing:* We published these particular parkings following the principles defined in [12] and using the Linked Time-Series Server [13]. We extended this implementation to support RML mapping rules, by just providing the mapping files as part of the server's configuration.

Fig. 3. Velopark-UI view for the region of Ghent, Belgium.

An example of the republished data containing the latest available observations for the city of Ghent, can be found at https://velopark.ilabt.imec.be/data/live/gent/. Furthermore, historic data can be accessed at https://velopark.ilabt.imec.be/data/live/gent/fragments and can be traversed by following the links defined by the `hydra:previous` predicate.

5   Conclusion and Future Work

The Velopark initiative brought together bicycle infrastructure experts from multiple organizations, all having overlapping interests. Promoting cycling as a main way of transportation and delivering relevant and reliable information to cyclists is a common denominator for these organizations. So far, 31 Belgian municipalities and 4 different BPMs have actively engaged into the Velopark platform, publishing data about 1599 parking facilities. To the best of our knowledge, this represents the most complete and open bicycle parking dataset in Belgium to this date. Furthermore, a third-party application, namely Hopper[18] is already reusing Velopark's data. Hopper is a route planning application designed to give route advise to electric bicycle users, in combination with public transport. Hopper uses data from Velopark to display which train stations have bicycle parkings.

Another important achievement from this project is the definition of a common data model for Bicycle parkings. By extending existing vocabularies such as Schema.org and MobiVoc, OVV aims for higher interoperability for bicycle parking data. In addition to follow the recommended best practices for publishing Linked Data on the Web, extending Schema.org was also motivated by achieving higher visibility of the data on search engines. Unfortunately, search engines like Google do not recognize external extensions to Schema.org out of

---

[18] https://openhopper.be/.

the box. This requires first OVV to go through the official extension recognition process of Schema.org, which is part of our future work.

Between the two different strategies to publish data supported by the Velopark platform, we found that organizations with no resources to publish and manage data on their own, were more receptive and have demonstrated higher interest in making their data visible through the platform. Organizations in charge of a high number of facilities were more interested on having automatic processes capable of mapping their data to the OVV model. This is understandable since manually describing hundreds of facilities can be time consuming.

Another interesting finding is related to the bicycle parking data owned by public transport companies. We found that both NMBS (Belgian railway company) and De Lijn (Flemish public transport), had extensive and in some cases very detailed data about their facilities, although not open. It is notable considering that both companies had already implemented Open Data platforms on their own. However it is worth mentioning that both companies were cooperative and worked together with the Velopark team to openly publish their data.

One common behavior across all the, so far, involved BPMs has been the reluctance to self-host the data created through the Velopark platform. Even organizations with Open Data platforms and websites about their facilities preferred to rely on the Velopark hosting to publish their data. One of the concerns that were raised by the BPMs to for example, embed JSON-LD snippets into their websites, was keeping it updated. If the data was updated BPMs needed to either manually update this script or develop a connection between the content of these scripts, the data displayed in the website and their back-end systems. Currently this is one of the main issues of decentralized data managing.

On future work, we will aim on extending OVV to cover other types of cycling infrastructure such as, bicycle sharing systems and exclusive cycling lanes.

Acknowledgements. The authors would like to thank the Federal government of Belgium for funding this project. Also extend our gratitude to all the organizations that cooperated and made this project possible.

References

1. Buehler, R.: Determinants of bicycle commuting in the Washington, DC region: the role of bicycle parking, cyclist showers, and free car parking at work. Transp. Res. Part D Transp. Environ. **17**(7), 525–531 (2012). https://doi.org/10.1016/j.trd.2012.06.003
2. Chen, P., Liu, Q., Sun, F.: Bicycle parking security and built environments. Transp. Res. Part D Transp. Environ. **62**, 169–178 (2018). https://doi.org/10.1016/j.trd.2018.02.020
3. Dimou, A., Vander Sande, M., Colpaert, P., Verborgh, R., Mannens, E., Van de Walle, R.: RML: a generic language for integrated RDF mappings of heterogeneous data. In: Bizer, C., Heath, T., Auer, S., Berners-Lee, T. (eds.) Proceedings of the 7th Workshop on Linked Data on the Web. CEUR Workshop Proceedings, vol. 1184, April 2014. http://ceur-ws.org/Vol-1184/ldow2014_paper_01.pdf

4. Ferster, C., Fischer, J., Manaugh, K., Nelson, T., Winters, M.: Using Open-StreetMap to inventory bicycle infrastructure: a comparison with open data from cities. Int. J. Sustain. Transp. **14**(1), 64–73 (2020). https://doi.org/10.1080/15568318.2018.1519746

5. Guha, R.V., Brickley, D., Macbeth, S.: Schema.org: evolution of structured data on the web. Commun. ACM **59**(2), 44–51 (2016). https://doi.org/10.1145/2844544

6. Handy, S., van Wee, B., Kroesen, M.: Promoting cycling for transport: research needs and challenges. Transp. Rev. **34**(1), 4–24 (2014). https://doi.org/10.1080/01441647.2013.860204

7. Heyvaert, P., De Meester, B., Dimou, A., Verborgh, R.: Declarative rules for linked data generation at your fingertips! In: Proceedings of the 15th ESWC: Posters and Demos (2018)

8. Liu, C., Tapani, A., Kristoffersson, I., Rydergren, C., Jonsson, D.: Development of a large-scale transport model with focus on cycling. Transp. Res. Part A Pol. Pract. **134**, 164–183 (2020). https://doi.org/10.1016/j.tra.2020.02.010

9. Lovejoy, K., Handy, S.: Developments in bicycle equipment and its role in promoting cycling as a travel mode. In: City Cycling. The MIT Press (10 2012). https://doi.org/10.7551/mitpress/9434.003.0008

10. Olbricht, R.M.: Data retrieval for small spatial regions in OpenStreetMap. In: Jokar Arsanjani, J., Zipf, A., Mooney, P., Helbich, M. (eds.) OpenStreetMap in GIScience. LNGC, pp. 101–122. Springer, Cham (2015). https://doi.org/10.1007/978-3-319-14280-7_6

11. Pucher, J., Buehler, R.: Making cycling irresistible: lessons from the Netherlands, Denmark and Germany. Transp. Rev. **28**(4), 495–528 (2008). https://doi.org/10.1080/01441640701806612

12. Rojas, J.A., Van de Vyvere, B., Gevaert, A., Taelman, R., Colpaert, P., Verborgh, R.: A preliminary open data publishing strategy for live data in Flanders. In: Companion Proceedings of the The Web Conference 2018, WWW 2018. pp. 1847–1853. International World Wide Web Conferences Steering Committee, Lyon, France (2018). https://doi.org/10.1145/3184558.3191650

13. Rojas Melendez, J.A., Sedrakyan, G., Colpaert, P., Vander Sande, M., Verborgh, R.: Supporting sustainable publishing and consuming of live linked time series streams. In: Gangemi, A., et al. (eds.) ESWC 2018. LNCS, vol. 11155, pp. 148–152. Springer, Cham (2018). https://doi.org/10.1007/978-3-319-98192-5_28

14. der Spek, S.C.V., Scheltema, N.: The importance of bicycle parking management. Res. Transp. Bus. Manage. **15**, 39–49 (2015). https://doi.org/10.1016/j.rtbm.2015.03.001. managing the Business of Cycling

15. Sun, S., Wang, B., Li, A.: Shared bicycle study to help reduce carbon emissions in Beijing. Energy Rep. **6**, 837–849 (2020). https://doi.org/10.1016/j.egyr.2019.11.017. The 6th International Conference on Energy and Environment Research - Energy and environment: challenges towards circular economy

How to Prototype a Client-Side Route Planner for Helsinki with Routable Tiles and Linked Connections

Julián Andrés Rojas$^{(\boxtimes)}$ⒾⒹ, Harm DelvaⒾⒹ, Pieter ColpaertⒾⒹ,
and Ruben VerborghⒾⒹ

IDLab, Department of Electronics and Information Systems,
Ghent University – imec, Ghent, Belgium
`julianandres.rojasmelendez@ugent.be`

Abstract. Route planning is key in application domains such as delivery services, tourism advice and ride sharing. Today's route planning as a service solutions do not cover all requirements of each use case, forcing application developers to build their own self-hosted route planners. This quickly becomes expensive to develop and maintain, especially when it requires integrating data from different sources. We demo a configurable route planner that takes advantage of strategically designed data publishing approaches and performs data integration and query execution on the client. For this demonstrator, we (i) publish a Linked Connections interface for the public transit data in Helsinki, including live updates; (ii) integrate Routable Tiles, a tiled Linked Data version of OpenStreetMap road network and (iii) implement a graphical user interface, on top of the Planner.js SDK we have built, to display the query results. By moving the data integration to the client, we provide higher flexibility for application developers to customize their solutions according to their needs. While the querying might be slow today, these preliminary results already hint at different data publishing strategies that may increase query evaluation performance on the client-side.

Keywords: Linked Data · Public transport · Linked Connections · Routable Tiles · Route planning

1 Introduction

Route planning is a key feature for application domains like delivery services, tourism advice or ride sharing. However, each use case has its own specific needs. For example, delivery services require detailed data about road networks and building entrances. Tourism websites require data about public transit alternatives and points of interest. Ride sharing services need to check for intermodality with other services. Currently available *route planning as a service* solutions

Available online at https://julianrojas.org/papers/sem4tra2020-demo.

I.-Y. Ko et al. (Eds.): ICWE 2020 Workshops, LNCS 12451, pp. 65–69, 2020.
https://doi.org/10.1007/978-3-030-65665-2_7

(e.g., Google Maps[1], CityMapper[2], etc.) do not offer a complete solution for every use case and, more importantly, do not allow extending their implementations to consider specific needs. This forces application developers to build their own self-hosted and custom tailored route planning solutions. Such self-hosted system quickly becomes expensive to develop and maintain, especially when it requires integrating heterogeneous data sources.

We consider this data integration problem an important bottleneck in setting up a route planner. We aim to lower the cost of prototyping a new route planner by automating the data integration from data sources published across the Web. To this end, we envision strategically designed Web APIs that allow route planning clients to access the relevant pieces of data they need to evaluate a particular query. The Linked Data principles [2] play a major role in the design of such Web APIs, as they facilitate data integration by reusing identifiers. Furthermore, we move data processing and query execution to the client side, allowing more flexibility for developers to tailor their implementations according to the specific needs of their use case. At its core is a Web engineering problem: how to design the Web APIs for automated querying?

This demo (available online[3]) illustrates our on-going work in automating data adoption in route planners. It introduces a new user interface built on top of an early release of our new Planner.js SDK[4]. We made it operational for the city of Helsinki, using data from Helsinki's public transit operator HSL[5] and OpenStreetMap, allowing browsers to calculate an attendee's way back to the hotel after the ICWE conference, if it would have taken place physically. Given a start URL provided by the users either at build or runtime, it can automatically find its way through a hypermedia structure to download the right fragments of the public transit schedules and road network data needed to answer route planning queries.

2   State of the Art

Route planning has been extensively studied throughout the years. Bast et al. [1] and Pajor [7] present an analysis of multiple route planning algorithms. Specialized software exists to calculate routes on road and transit networks. These can be categorized in: (i) software as a service, (ii) self-hosted server software, and (iii) client-side route planners. Software as a service that can be used for route planning includes Mapbox turn-by-turn[6], Google Maps or Navitia.io[7]. This approach is only customizable to the extent the service-provider allows customizing the route planning queries. Open-source tools to set up a route planner on

---

[1] https://cloud.google.com/maps-platform/routes/.
[2] https://citymapper.com/tools/1063/api-for-robots.
[3] http://193.190.127.152/plannerjs-demo.
[4] https://github.com/openplannerteam/planner-example.
[5] https://www.hsl.fi/en.
[6] https://www.mapbox.com/use-cases/turn-by-turn-navigation/.
[7] https://navitia.io.

your own server include Open Trip Planner[8], OSRM[9], or Itinero[10]. This approach requires to set up robust server infrastructure and deal with data integration processes, increasing operation and maintenance costs for application developers.

A third approach is a client-side route planner. An early version of a Software Development Kit (SKD) called Planner.js is used in this demo. The SDK currently works for Belgian public transport data [4], and world-wide short road network queries with a republished version of OpenStreetMap (OSM) as Routable Tiles [3].

In previous work, we presented an evaluation of a hypermedia driven Web API for public transit time schedules [4]. We did back then not yet have a way to calculate road network routes, and thus also no way of combining footpath transfers with the public transit time schedules. For calculating how to traverse road networks and how to calculate transfers between public transit alternatives, we introduced Routable Tiles [3]. This is a translation of all the roads from OSM to tile set similar to the slippy map URL template[11].

3   Planner.js for Helsinki

To make a tweakable Planner.js operational in Helsinki, we had to take two steps: (i) republish the Public Transit data of Helsinki as Linked Connections; and (ii) make a specific end-user road network profile for Helsinki that can be used by Planner.js.

The Public Transit Network - We took the open datasets of Helsinki's public transit operator HSL, and translated these data from the General Transit Feed Specification (GTFS[12] and GTFS-RT[13]) into Linked Connections. We set up a server connected to these GTFS and GTFS-RT feeds, exposing the corresponding Linked Connections interface[14]. Additionally, the server exposes the Routes and Stops defined in the transit network.

The Road Network - For Helsinki's road network, we reused previously published Routable Tiles[15] derived from OSM. Also, we published a pedestrian road network profile[16] and configured Planner.js to use it to calculated road-based routes.

The majority of the effort for building this route planner for Helsinki, was dedicated mostly to develop the user interface. Converting and publishing the

---

[8] http://opentripplanner.org.
[9] http://project-osrm.org/.
[10] https://itinero.tech.
[11] https://wiki.openstreetmap.org/wiki/Slippy_Map.
[12] https://developers.google.com/transit/gtfs/reference.
[13] https://developers.google.com/transit/gtfs-realtime/reference.
[14] https://icwe.julianrojas.org/hsl/connections.
[15] https://tiles.openplanner.team/planet/14/9326/4743.
[16] https://hdelva.be/profile/pedestrian.

public transit data was simplified by using the Linked Connections Server[17]. Integrating road network data was handled automatically by Planner.js. This shows that once data has been published and made accessible through an appropriate Web API, application developers could dedicate most of their effort on improving their applications and providing a better service to their users, instead of on data integration tasks.

4   Demonstrator

In this demo (see Fig. 1), the users are able to choose between a *Flexible Road Planner* for road only route planning and a *Flexible Transit Planner* for road and transit route planning. Additionally to Helsinki's data, users are able to include more public transit datasources. This demo includes a list with our previously published sources from Belgium, but users may include their own. The demo is available online at https://icwe.julianrojas.org/plannerjs-demo).

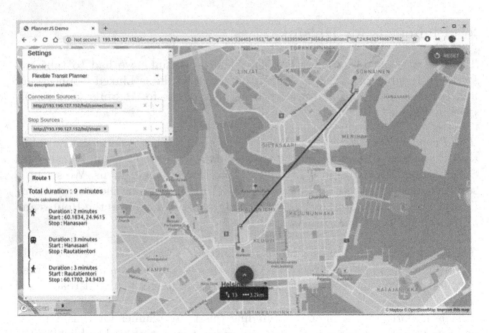

Fig. 1. Demo application showing Planner.js functional in the region of Helsinki

5   Conclusion and Future Work

The benefits of this approach are: (i) full flexiblity for reusers: they can implement the algorithm they want, while always having the latest data; and (ii) cheaper to host transport datasets for data publishers.

---

[17] https://github.com/linkedconnections/linked-connections-server.

The drawback of this approach is that it may perform more slowly than server-based solutions and it will need to download a high volume of data when the Linked Data APIs are not well fragmented for the specific query. However, reusers do not need to maintain their own server and can keep their applications online using a simple file host. On-going work is making Planner.js work faster, by offering the client better preprocessed data to work with [5,6]. Clients will be able to pick the right source, also based on what source would give the fastest response to a certain query. Therefore, we will also be working on further automating the discovery of sources from a catalog instead of always mentioning the precise dataset.

We hope this early demo stimulates other researchers and open transport advocates to apply Linked Connections on the open data from their region. With the project Linked OpenStreetMap[18] we will gather all our projects on republishing OSM as Linked Data, and hope also other contributors will join in to make OSM queryable from the client-side. We also hope that HSL will start publishing persistent identifiers and global URIs for e.g., their stops, connections, trips, routes and lines, such that integration of their data with other datasets can be automated and remain valid over time.

References

1. Bast, H., et al.: Route planning in transportation networks. CoRR abs/1504.05140 (2015), http://arxiv.org/abs/1504.05140
2. Berners-Lee, T., Hendler, J., Lassila, O., et al.: The semantic web. Sci. Am. **284**(5), 28–37 (2001)
3. Colpaert, P., Abelshausen, B., Meléndez, J.A.R., Delva, H., Verborgh, R.: Republishing OpenStreetMap's roads as linked routable tiles. In: Hitzler, P., et al. (eds.) ESWC 2019. LNCS, vol. 11762, pp. 13–17. Springer, Cham (2019). https://doi.org/10.1007/978-3-030-32327-1_3
4. Colpaert, P., Verborgh, R., Mannens, E.: Public transit route planning through lightweight linked data interfaces. In: Cabot, J., De Virgilio, R., Torlone, R. (eds.) ICWE 2017. LNCS, vol. 10360, pp. 403–411. Springer, Cham (2017). https://doi.org/10.1007/978-3-319-60131-1_26
5. Delva, H., Rojas Melendez, J.A., Abelshausen, B., Colpaert, P., Verborgh, R.: Client-side route planning: preprocessing the OpenStreetMap road network for routable tiles. In: Academic Track, State of the Map 2019, pp. 23–24. Ghent University (2019). https://hdelva.be/slides/sotm2019/
6. Delva, H., Rojas Melendez, J.A., Colpaert, P., Verborgh, R.: Decentralized publication and consumption of transfer footpaths. In: First International Workshop on Semantics for Transport, vol. 2447, pp. 1–7 (2019). https://hdelva.be/slides/sem1tra2010/#/
7. Pajor, T.: Algorithm Engineering for Realistic Journey Planning in Transportation Networks. Ph.D. thesis, Karlsruhe Institute of Technology (2013). https://d-nb.info/1058165240/34

---

[18] https://losm.org.

6th International Workshop on Knowledge Discovery on the Web (KDWEB 2020)

6th International Workshop on Knowledge Discovery on the Web (KDWEB 2020)

The Sixth edition of the International Workshop on Knowledge Discovery on the Web was a satellite event of the International Conference on Web Engineering for the third time after the previous successful coordination of the events in 2018 and 2019.

KDWEB focuses on the field of Knowledge Discovery using digital data, with particular attention to Data Mining, Machine Learning, and Information Retrieval methods, systems, and applications. The aim of KDWEB is to provide a venue for researchers, scientists, students, and practitioners involved in the fields of Knowledge Discovery, Data Mining, Information Retrieval, and the Semantic Web, to present and discuss novel and emerging ideas.

This year, we received only one paper, which can be attributed to the COVID-19 pandemic as an extraordinary global public health issue and that research activities were significantly impacted.

Nevertheless, KDWEB 2020 has been accepted for the ICWE 2020 workshop joint session. We are grateful to the ICWE 2020 organizers for the support and the coordination of the session.

The accepted paper is titled "Research on Standardization Technology of Software Testing Process Based on Workflow," and authored by Nan Li, Qiang Han, Yu He, Cong Liu, Zijian Mao, Haide Liu, and Yichen Wang. They propose a tool to manage and control the testing process, and adopt standardized technology management to avoid the interference of unreliable factors and to make the testing process more standardized. The quality of the presented paper and its value is high, and the overall discussion provided by the authors within the workshop has shown the importance of the theme in the community of Web engineering.

November 2020

Giuliano Armano
Matteo Cristani
Alessandro Giuliani

KDWEB 2019 Organization

Workshop Chairs

Giuliano Armano   University of Cagliari, Italy
Matteo Cristani   University of Verona, Italy
Alessandro Giuliani University of Cagliari, Italy

Publication Chair

Alessandro Bozzon   Delft University of Technology, The Netherlands

Publicity Chair

Claudio Tomazzoli   University of Cagliari, Italy

Research on Standardization Technology of Software Testing Process Based on Workflow

Nan Li, Qiang Han[✉], Yu He, Cong Liu, Zijian Mao, Haide Liu, and Yichen Wang

School of Computer Science and Engineering, North Minzu University, Yinchuan 750021, China
hanqiang@nmu.edu.cn

Abstract. Software testing is an important means to ensure software quality, and one of the most important attributes of software quality is software reliability. By eliminating the errors and defects found in the testing process, the reliability level can be effectively improved. Based on the existing software reliability model, a standardized technology for software testing process is proposed. Firstly, compare the current typical software reliability models, capture their commonalities, analyze the software testing process of the model, and add standardized technology on this basis to strictly control the testing process. Secondly, a modeling process with architectural standards is formed, continually improve and optimize the model to further improve the accuracy of detecting errors and defects, and combine the workflow technology to analyze and study the software testing process management. Finally, a standardized workflow testing mechanism is established to shorten the testing cycle while continuously improving software quality. This paper, based on workflow technology of jBPM platform and combined with Web access method, proposes a method of implementation and deployment of various software testing processes that conform to common standards.

Keywords: Software testing · Reliability model · Standardized technology · jBPM · Web · Workflow

1 Introduction

Software testing is an evaluation method for software products. The main purpose is to find errors in the software, that is, errors or malfunctions caused in the behavior of software programs or software applications. Test cases are used by testers to verify whether the system under test is working properly. The development of test cases is helpful to find the gaps or requirements of the application [1].

Software reliability testing technology is very important for improving, ensuring, evaluating and verifying the reliability of software [2]. Through reasonable and correct testing, the software quality can be effectively predicted and improved. The improvement of software quality should not be limited to the technology and method of software testing. Although many advanced testing techniques have been proposed, the testing effect still need to be improved. Therefore, scientific and effective testing specifications are very important to prevent problems such as the ambiguity of tester positions and not

© Springer Nature Switzerland AG 2020
I.-Y. Ko et al. (Eds.): ICWE 2020 Workshops, LNCS 12451, pp. 75–86, 2020.
https://doi.org/10.1007/978-3-030-65665-2_8

strictly observing software test standards. As a result, after a certain amount of testing, the software quality is not high. In fact, the standardized management and control of software testing process can improve its quality more effectively.

Workflow is a part or whole automation of business process in computer application environment. It is an abstract description of business processes and work processes [3], so that the process can be executed in the prescribed order. And workflow standardization further highlights the advantages of workflow, the standardization technology is applied to the workflow platform to realize the standardization and efficiency of business process.

In this paper, based on the workflow technology of jBPM platform and combined with the Web access method, we propose a method of implementation and deployment of various software testing processes that conform to common standards. Based on the data information obtained through the whole testing process, the reliability model is used to analyze these data, and mining out the key technologies that can improve the quality of software. By analyzing different classical reliability models, a standardized software testing process is extracted and managed by jBPM platform to ensure the automation and standardization of software testing process.

The structure of this article is as follows: in Sect. 2, we outline related work. In Sect. 3, we describe the key technologies used in the testing process, such as Web technology and jBPM technology. In Sect. 4, we summarize the testing process mentioned above and analyze a standardized testing process, and describe the specific deployment method of this process. Finally, Sect. 5 provides our conclusions and future research directions.

2   Related Work

Software reliability modeling usually proposes a model hypothesis, and then measures the output of the model, which estimates the value of the parameter by a certain method, and finally enters the data to verify the final result. A reasonable and accurate model is established based on the two technologies of model development and prediction to ensure that software reliability has a place in the entire system. The diagram of software reliability system schematic is shown in Fig. 1 [4]. The ultimate goal is to control software quality by generating better procedure. In this part, we mainly introduce the software testing process and the data analysis process of the following two models.

2.1   Software Testing Process

In order to better compare and analyze the following two models, we get the data information of model input through software testing. The corresponding error report is generated during the entire testing process, including the total number of errors found, error types, interval between two failures and other information, which lays a good foundation for the standardized testing process mentioned below. The specific testing process is shown in Fig. 2.

2.2   Jelinski-Moranda Model

The Jelinski-Moranda (J-M) model is also a Markov process and is considered to be the earliest software reliability model developed by Jelinski and Moranda. It has strongly influenced many later models which are actually modifications of this simple model [5].

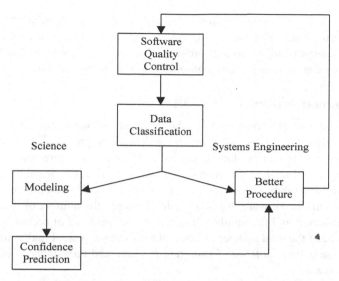

Fig. 1. Software reliability system schematic.

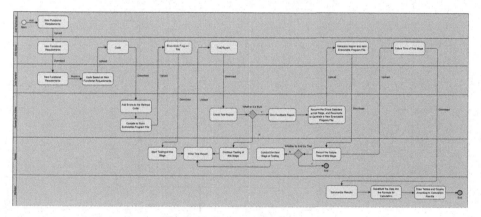

Fig. 2. Software testing process.

First, the basic assumptions are put forward as follows:

1) The total number of errors in the software is N.
2) The failure rate of a software system is directly proportional to the number of errors in the software at all times, proportionality constant is φ. It is subject to Poisson distribution.
3) When an error is found during the test, it is immediately eliminated and N is reduced by one.

In [6], the J-M model considers that the interval from the $i-1$ times failure to the i times failure is a random variable that follows the exponential distribution with

$Z(x_i) = \varphi[N - (i - 1)]$ as the parameter. Among them, $Z(x_i)$ represents the failure rate of each test error, and the failure rate φ in the formula and the error number N in the software are estimated to obtain the software reliability. Here, we counted the interval time corresponding to 31 defects that have been found during the test.

2.3 Hypergeometric Distribution Model

Hypergeometric distribution model is used to estimate the number of inherent errors in the program at the beginning of the testing or debugging process [7]. It can estimate software reliability by adding human errors. First define a failure rate formula, and use the experimental results of this model to estimate the value of the proportionality constant. Then, according to the total number of errors added manually, the number of inherent errors in the software, the relationship between the number of inherent errors in software detected and the number of human errors detected at present to obtain an estimated value of the total number of inherent errors in software. Finally, substitute the estimated value into the software failure rate formula, and then analyze the quality of the current software.

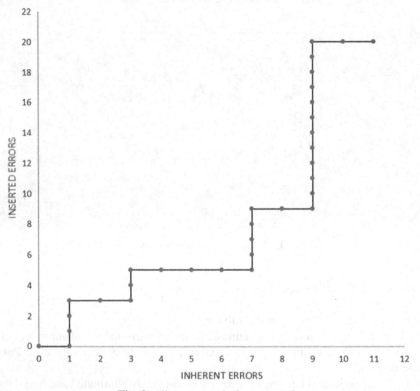

Fig. 3. History record of error search.

In this model, we analyze software reliability by counting the frequency of these two types of errors occurred. Figure 3 shows the relationship between the number of inherent errors in the software and the number of human inserted errors, in which each error is found, the value of the corresponding coordinate will be increased by one correspondingly.

2.4 Model Analysis

Both of the above models can be used to estimate and predict the number of errors in software, and ultimately achieve the purpose of improving software quality. However, the process of data input into the model is artificially controlled. For example, when running the Jelinski-Moranda model to output data, because the total number of errors estimated in certain stages exceeds the expected value. Therefore, a threshold was artificially set during the testing process to terminate the data output, resulting in differences in the calculation results at some stages. Our innovation is to apply the standardized technology to the reliability testing process, to prevent human factors from interfering with the data value, and to help improve the quality of software testing. Figure 4 shows the comparison of the total number of defects currently estimated by the two models at each stage with the addition of human errors.

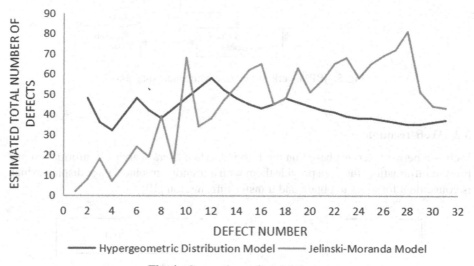

Fig. 4. Comparison of total defects.

3 System Architecture

In this section, we introduced the key technologies of standardized management and control tool proposed to standardize the software reliability testing process, which are necessary support for improving software reliability.

3.1 jBPM Technology

jBPM is an open-source workflow framework, which is applicable to various process specifications and has flexible and extensible properties. It provides functions such as process definition, process deployment, process execution and management, which can simplify the programming process [8]. The business process designer completes process definition by calling the process definition interface of the engine, and saves the defined data to the database. The process monitoring tool manages and controls the running process by calling the interface of the workflow. As shown in Fig. 5 [9].

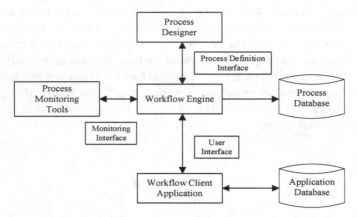

Fig. 5. jBPM workflow engine component diagram.

3.2 Web Technology

Web is a network service based on the Internet, when users search for information and browse information, they can provide them with a friendly graphical page display, which is convenient for users to obtain and transfer information [10].

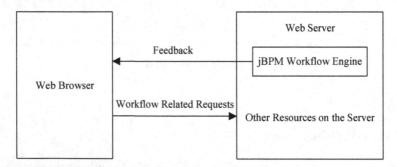

Fig. 6. Web access to jBPM workflow engine.

Taking the workflow software testing process as an example. The user requests a workflow resource from the Web server on the Web browser. After the Web server receives the request, it finds that the resource belongs to the jBPM workflow engine, performs the current requested test task, and feeds back the results of the jBPM workflow engine to the browser. Accessing the jBPM workflow engine through a Web browser as shown in Fig. 6.

4 Standardization of Testing Process

Standardization of the software testing process helps to improve the quality and effi-ciency of software testing, thereby promoting the standardization of the software devel-opment process and improve the quality of products. The testing process should have the characteristics of standardization, order, systematic and engineering. The application of relevant management tools can provide correct guidance, organization and implemen-tation, so as to continuously improve the quality of software, and ultimately improve customer satisfaction [11].

4.1 Standardization Technology Research

It is extremely important to introduce standardized ideas in the reliability testing process to ensure software quality, in essence to obtain the best order of the testing process. Although the traditional reliability testing methods can find errors in the software to a certain extent, but its testing methods have the disadvantages of low efficiency, high cost and poor universality. Moreover, it may introduce human input errors in the non-standard software testing process, which reduces the software quality. In order to finally evaluate whether the software system has good application value, determine whether the product achieves the reliability purpose, modify and analyze the part where the failure is detected [12].

Standards are static text content, which stipulates software quality models and puts forward the basis for quality requirements. Standardization is a series of activities carried out around standards. It is an important carrier for the promotion of new technologies, an application path for technological innovation, and an effective tool for establishing the best order. Its corresponding standardization technology is the core content of this article. In order to solve the generalization of complex models, we have built a standardized software testing process to achieve the purpose of effectively managing and controlling the input of different types of models.

4.2 Testing Process Analysis

The software reliability model defines a random process that describes the behavior of software errors with respect to time [13]. In the process of reliability testing, these models are used to access current and future reliability for a period of time to achieve the purpose of improving software quality [14].

Software reliability model has been continuously optimized, at present, there are also many types of existing models, such as reliability growth model, the non-homogeneous poisson process model, input the domain class model. They both have in common and differences. The Jelinski-Moranda model allows the failure rate to decrease in a discrete form. Then according to the maximum likelihood estimation method estimates the parameter values of the model. Through continuous testing to eliminate the faults in the software, the reliability will increase with time [15]. The hypergeometric distribution model adds human errors, establishes the relationship between human errors and inherent errors, and applies the idea of extremum to obtain the number of inherent errors in the software.

The above two models are similar in the main idea of reliability testing. Both input test data, estimate model parameters, and finally give a reliability evaluation of software quality, that is, an output. What is important is how to further improve and guarantee the quality of software based on the existing software reliability model. The most effective and economical method is to adopt certain technical means for reliability testing control. To standardize the testing process, it is necessary to establish a standardized reliability testing process. Based on the above two models, it is mainly to design a tool to manage the testing process, follow the unified testing principle, and prevent the model from illegally inputting human errors and affecting the software reliability.

4.3 Testing Process Deployment

Here, we propose a method for implementing and deploying a variety of software testing processes based on the Web and jBPM platforms. In the face of a wide variety of software reliability testing models, a unified modeling process is defined. The business process for software reliability testing is drawn through the process designer as shown in Fig. 7.

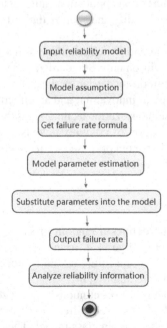

Fig. 7. Reliability testing process.

In order to better improve the quality of software, it is necessary to use standardized technology to control the entire testing process. Then the standardized methods are used to control these two models respectively, which is characterized by generalizing the models into two types and simplifying complex types of software reliability models, making the testing process less susceptible to external interference, and the output software failure rate is more accurate, thereby effectively improving software quality.

In order to standardize the testing process, it is necessary to build a jBPM development environment, and deploy a test process management tool based on jBPM technology to an application server, so as to serve access, monitoring, and management from the Web. The front end is used to display the human-computer interaction interface, and the back end is used to implement the deployment of the reliability testing process. From the perspective of software testing, using workflow technology to establish a relatively standardized testing mechanism can effectively improve the efficiency of testing.

jBPM is a business process management framework based on the java language, which mainly includes a workflow engine and a graphical process designer based on the eclipse platform. The jBPM workflow engine uses 18 database tables. These databases are used to record workflow information such as user names, user group relationships, current tasks, current process variables, historical tasks, and historical process variables. The workflow engine implements operations on these database tables through the hibernate module [16]. The specific process is to first design the process according to the functional relationship to get the information of each task node, then visualize the database through navicat, create a new database, then need to deploy the process design on jBPM. Finally, publish the process to 18 database tables to generate the corresponding workflow information. The data used for model analysis in this paper comes from the software testing process. Figure 8 shows the detailed execution process of the test task node. The detailed data information is obtained according to the uploaded test errors report, and then input it into the model to analyze its reliability. In this process, compare the output results of different models, analyze the reasons, and finally establish a standardized testing process based on the jBPM platform.

DBID	CLASS	DBVERSION	HPROCI	TYPE	EXECUTION	ACTIVITY_NAME	START	END
10003	task		1	10001	task	Test_Process.10001	Add Errors to the Refined Code	2020-06-12 10:25:05	2020-06-12 10:29:25
20002	task		1	10001	task	Test_Process.10001	Compile into Executable Program File	2020-06-12 10:29:26	2020-06-12 10:35:48
30002	task		1	10001	task	Test_Process.10001	Upload Executable Program File	2020-06-12 10:35:48	2020-06-12 10:37:40
40002	task		1	10001	task	Test_Process.10001	Start Testing at this Stage	2020-06-12 10:37:40	2020-06-12 10:39:02
50002	task		1	10001	task	Test_Process.10001	Write Test Report	2020-06-12 10:39:02	2020-06-12 10:39:35
60002	task		1	10001	task	Test_Process.10001	Upload Test Report	2020-06-12 10:39:35	2020-06-12 10:40:09
70002	task		1	10001	task	Test_Process.10001	Check Test Report	2020-06-12 10:40:10	2020-06-12 10:41:18
80001	excl		0	10001	decision	Test_Process.10001	Whether it is BUG	2020-06-12 10:41:18	2020-06-12 10:41:18
80003	task		1	10001	task	Test_Process.10001	Give Feedback Report	2020-06-12 10:41:18	2020-06-12 10:42:00
90002	task		1	10001	task	Test_Process.10001	Remove the errors Detected at this Stage	2020-06-12 10:42:00	2020-06-12 10:43:06
100002	task		1	10001	task	Test_Process.10001	Recompile to Generate a New Executable Program File	2020-06-12 10:43:06	2020-06-12 10:43:31
110002	task		1	10001	task	Test_Process.10001	Upload Feedback Report and New Executable Program File	2020-06-12 10:43:31	2020-06-12 10:44:11
120002	task		1	10001	task	Test_Process.10001	Record the Failure Time of this Stage	2020-06-12 10:44:11	2020-06-12 10:44:46
130002	task		1	10001	task	Test_Process.10001	Substitute the Data into the Formula for Calculation	2020-06-12 10:44:46	2020-06-12 10:45:06
140002	task		1	10001	task	Test_Process.10001	Draw Tables and Graphs According to Calculation Results	2020-06-12 10:45:06	2020-06-12 10:45:24
150001	excl		0	10001	decision	Test_Process.10001	exclusive1	2020-06-12 10:45:24	2020-06-12 10:45:24

Fig. 8. The execution process of software testing.

4.4 Web Access

The Web access for the implementation of the software testing process is mainly based on B/S access, including client access, Web application server, database, etc. Combined with the Web access method, it provides users with real interactive ability, which can better reflect the standard testing process through the interface, Fig. 9 is the interface of Web access to standardized testing process. There are two models available for selection here, one is the hypergeometric distribution model, and the other is the Jelinski-Moranda model, the selected model will be grayed out.

The interface can show the entire testing process, which is a standard and unified modeling process mentioned above, that is, the business process of reliability testing. Every time a button is clicked, the background running program is started, and the failure rate value can be output through calculation, and then the software reliability can be obtained. Then, the software quality can be effectively improved by modifying the errors found in the software. At the bottom of the interface is the visualization of the probability density of the Jelinski-Moranda model. Through the way of interface display can more intuitively and vividly represent the software failure rate, which is helpful to analyze the software reliability.

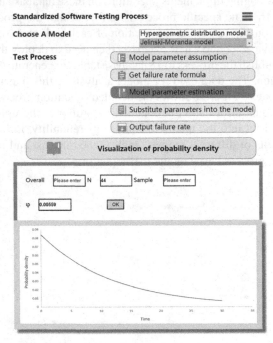

Fig. 9. Web standardized testing business process.

5   Conclusion

Nowadays, software reliability models are widely used by testers, but not all testers can test according to standardized procedures. In this paper, we propose a tool to manage and control the testing process, and adopt standardized technology management to avoid the interference of unreliable factors and make the testing process more standardized. In particular, most software reliability models can be controlled and reflected through the Web access method. Finally, the relevant software reliability information is output, the faults in the software are found and modified, and the software reliability is continuously improved.

In the future, we will add more classic software reliability growth models. Because different software needs to choose different models for reliability prediction, in order to standardize the testing process, we need to establish a unified testing process that can meet most of the classical software reliability models. Finally, combined with standardized technology to uniformly manage the reliability testing process to achieve the effect of managing and controlling most reliability growth models, it can effectively improve the accuracy of model reliability testing and lay a solid foundation for improving software quality.

References

1. Sneha, K., Malle, G.M.: Research on software testing techniques and software automation testing tools. In: 2017 International Conference on Energy, Communication, Data Analytics and Soft Computing (ICECDS), Chennai, pp. 77–81 (2017)
2. Liu, C., Ren, Z., Li, H., Liu, Y.: Software reliability testing in practice: an industry case study with a typical airborne software system. In: 2014 10th International Conference on Reliability, Maintainability and Safety (ICRMS), Guangzhou, pp. 363–368 (2014)
3. Jiang, H.: Research and implementation of financial approval system based on jBPM engine. In: 2018 IEEE 3rd Advanced Information Technology, Electronic and Automation Control Conference (IAEAC), Chongqing, pp. 394–399 (2018)
4. Jelinski, Z., Moranda, P.: Software Reliability Research (1972). https://doi.org/10.1016/B978-0-12-266950-7.50028-1
5. Luo, Z., Cao, P., Tang, G., Wu, L.: A modification to the Jelinski-Moranda software reliability growth model based on cloud model theory. In: 2011 Seventh International Conference on Computational Intelligence and Security, Hainan, pp. 195–198 (2011)
6. Che, J., Zhou, L.: Research and progress of software reliability model. Comput. Digit. Eng. **46**(12), 2430–2434+2441 (2018)
7. Tohma, Y., Yamano, H., Ohba, M., Jacoby, R.: The estimation of parameters of the hypergeometric distribution and its application to the software reliability growth model. IEEE Trans. Softw. Eng. **17**(5), 483–489 (1991)
8. Hailan, P., Wenrong, J., Shiwei, L.: Research on collaboration software based on JBPM and lightweight J2EE Framework. In: 2010 International Conference on E-Business and E-Government, Guangzhou, pp. 191–194 (2010)
9. Bing, H., Dan-Mei, X.: Research and design of document flow model based on JBPM workflow engine. In: 2009 International Forum on Computer Science-Technology and Applications, Chongqing, pp. 336–339 (2009)

10. Tala, Song, M., Zhang, X., Xu, H., Song, J.: A solution of web services combination based on JBPM. In: 2009 IEEE International Symposium on IT in Medicine & Education, Jinan, pp. 421–426 (2009)
11. Li, W., Hao, Z.: FPGA software testing process management. In: 2015 IEEE International Conference on Grey Systems and Intelligent Services (GSIS), Leicester, pp. 600–603 (2015)
12. Liu, C., Huang, Z., Chen, L.: Software Evaluator Course, pp. 73–76. Tsinghua University Press, Beijing (2005)
13. Lyu, M.: Software reliability engineering: a roadmap. In: FoSE 2007: Future of Software Engineering, pp. 153–170. https://doi.org/10.1109/fose.2007.24
14. Kaswan, K.S, Choudhary, S, Sharma, K.: 5unified software development process based classification of software reliability models. In: International Conference on Computing for Sustainable Global Development. IEEE (2015)
15. Miyakwa, O., Tohma, Y.: Software reliability evaluation service operation. Syst. Comput. Jpn. 38(1), 97–104 (2007)
16. Zhu, C., Wang, X., Yin, Z.: Application research of JBPM4 workflow engine in scientific research project management system. Electron. Technol. Softw. Eng. 01, 193–195 (2017)

Author Index

Printed in the United States
By Bookmasters